A Musical History of the Klamath Basin
Early Community Bands

TABLE OF CONTENTS

Introduction: Intersection of History and Musical Practice   5

Part 1: Klamath Falls Community Bands   9
    Early Music (Fort Klamath, Linkville Orchestra)   9
    Brass Band   13
    Klamath Falls Military Band   17
    Klamath Falls Municipal Band   47

Part 2: Social Organization Bands   69
    Shriners   71
    Elks   77
    Eagles   85
    American Legion   93

Part 3: Bands from Outlying Communities   113
    Merrill   115
    Malin   117
    Fort Klamath   118
    Dorris   119
    Bonanza   121
    Klamath Agency   122
    Keno   123

Conclusion: The Importance of Local Bands in Community Development   125

Introduction:
The Intersection of History and Musical Practice

It is a common trope that music does not exist in a vacuum. Rather, music typically reflects the social and cultural conditions in which it is created. This book attempts to provide an overview of early Klamath County history using music as a focal point to study and understand various stages of Klamath's past. The result is a decent general overview of major historical episodes in the Klamath Basin with specific details about Klamath's musical history and legacy.

Music and music making can take many different forms. The Klamath Basin has been home to a wide variety of music, from community efforts all the way to high profile and professional events. Though this musical history exists on a wide spectrum, each sample of music tells us something about Klamath's colorful history.

Music is a field where culture, history, community, and so many other facets of our lives meet. It can provide a soundtrack for our history, allowing us to learn more about the past with more than just images or words.

In the Klamath Basin, music held a prominent position in the community. Many of the community groups established over time did so much more than simply entertain. Rather, these groups played an important role in the social and economic development of the area. Klamath leaders recognized that a thriving arts scene would increase the visibility and attractiveness of the community. Throughout Klamath's early history, community leaders constantly sent local music groups on trips to a wide variety of competitions and events to advertise and show off the Klamath community.

A note about the groups included in this book: Klamath has been home to a wealth of musical talent since its beginning. As such, there have been countless local music groups throughout the history of this region, and it would be very difficult to cover all of these groups in detail. Rather, this book focuses more on groups that played integral roles in the socioeconomic development of the community, especially when these groups were well-documented and in operation for a substantial number of years.

This book comes from nearly seven years of accumulating sources during my time as the Curator of the Klamath County Museums. Special thanks are due to museum volunteer Dave Mattos for his help with research and newspaper scanning, to Carol Mattos for her help with research, to Kristen Sonniksen for her help with formatting, and to Miran Reynolds for editing. In order to make the project more manageable, I chose to terminate the focus of this book in the 1960s. Future projects may focus on later musical groups.

Klamath Star May 9, 1895:
NOT UP ON BAND DISCIPLINE

Gen. Schofield's Criticism of Sousa's Famous Musical Aggregation. Conductor Sousa was taken to task by Gen. Schofield for his lack of discipline and it is explained by the San Francisco Chronicle. The last echo of one of Sousa's overtures was just dying away over the hills south of the fairgrounds, when Gen. Schofield stepped in front of the band and saluted the distinguished leader. Sousa returned the salute and sent one of his men to escort the general up into the band stand.

"That music was beautiful," exclaimed the general, as he took Sousa's hand warmly, "I am astonished, sir, that you get such results with so little discipline."

There is nothing that Sousa prides himself more on that being one of the strictest disciplinarians, and he was naturally nettled at the general's criticism.

"Why, general, my men are under perfect control. I'm sure they are thoroughly drilled and I can hardly believe that there is any lack of discipline: I have never noticed it!"

"No, that's just it: you don't see it," persisted the general, "I saw it though. Do you know as soon as you turn your back on one side of your band to shake your baton on the other, those fellows all quit playing. Of course you don't see it, for as soon as you turn around they begin again!"

Early Music in the Klamath Basin

The earliest examples of Western music in the Klamath Basin undoubtedly come from the early explorers and pioneers who moved into the region. Though we do not have much documentation about these musical occurrences, we can extrapolate some information based on some resources that have survived to this day.

The establishment of Fort Klamath in 1863 marked the first significant white settlement in the Klamath area. With the fort came the bugle calls and music stemming from an already established military music tradition in the United States. The music was practical for communication, but it eventually took on more cultural and historical significance as well.

Archaeological work completed on the historical Fort Klamath site in 2014-2015 uncovered fragments of a 1800s vintage trumpet, suggesting that the bugle tradition was alive and well at Fort Klamath.

One of the first documented and organized music groups in the area that we know about was the Linkville Orchestra. Most of what we know about this group comes from a single photo of the band, which lists the names of the band members on the back.

1800s trumpet pieces recovered from Fort Creek in 2014

The members included Milan Loosely on clarinet, John Verlings on a valve trombone, John Houston on double bass, Will Bondoin on cornet, J.T. Butcher on 1st violin, and George R. Hurn on 2nd violin. Hurn would go on to be active in other musical groups in Klamath Falls, including the Klamath Falls Military Band. The picture notes that Milan Loosely would go on to join the Washington Marine Band.

This group would morph into the Klamath Falls Orchestra, which hosted a number of events and concerts around town. They also started the tradition of steamboat excursions on Upper Klamath. (Klamath Republican, 06-05-1902; Klamath Republican, 11-13-1902; Klamath Republican 12-04-1902; Klamath Republican, 01-08-1903; Klamath Republican, 02-26-1903)

The Linkville Orchestra circa 1890
Klamath County Museum 192g8b

Klamath Falls would continue to have local orchestras throughout its history, but these groups, which mostly provided music for dances and similar events, will not be covered in this book. For a number of years at the turn of the century, however, the Klamath Falls Orchestra truly served in a similar fashion as a community band (Klamath Republican, 02-24-1904; Klamath Republican, 10-12-1905).

Klamath Falls Brass Band

Perhaps the first true community "band" in the Klamath area was the Klamath Falls Brass Band, which first appeared in local newspapers at the end of 1899 advertising a New Year's Day concert (Klamath Republican, 12-28-1899). The band performed many of their concerts at Houston's Opera House (Klamath Republican, 03-22-1900).

Houston's Opera House
Klamath County Museum 0015.1973.008.0800

In 1900, the Klamath Falls Brass Band organized festivities for a grand Fourth of July celebration in Klamath Falls. The event included a parade, baseball game, foot races, and a grand ball hosted by the band in the evening (Klamath Republican, 06-05-1900).

The Klamath Falls Brass Band performed for a number of dances, social events, parades, and celebrations, and they even brought their concerts to some of the outlying communities (Klamath Republican, 04-24-1902; Klamath Republican, 08-27-1903). They were often the main feature at Fourth of July celebrations and the local fair (Klamath Republican, 07-06-1905; Klamath Republican, 08-31-1905). They also performed during holidays (Klamath Republican, 12-21-1905).

In 1906, the local band would organize and adopt the name "Klamath Falls Military Band," though some sources still sometimes referred to them as the Klamath Falls Brass Band.

PROGRAM

JULY 4th, 1900,

AT

Klamath Falls, Ore.,

Under the Management of the

Klamath Falls Brass Band:

10 A. M., Parade.
10:30 A. M., Exercises at the Court House Grove.
1. Music by Band.
2. Prayer by Rev. C. E. Stockwell.
3. Song, "Hail Columbia," by Double Quartette.
4. Music by Band.
5. Recitation, "Flower of Liberty," by Miss Mamie Boyd.
6. Music by Band.
7. Oration by Robert A. Hopkins.
8. Song, "1776," by Double Quartette.

AMUSEMENT PROGRAM:

1. Foot race for boys under 14 years, 50 yards; prize, sweater given by I. A. Duffy.
2. Sack race, 50 yards; prize, $2.00.
3. Foot race, 100 yards, free for all; prize, $5.00.
4. Foot race for girls, 50 yards; prize, one dozen photographs given by Kelley.
5. Three legged race, 50 yards; prize, $2.00.
6. Wheelbarrow race for boys under 18 years, 25 yards, runners to be blindfolded and turn stake; first prize, $2; second prize, fine suit of Balbriggan underwear given by Racket Store.

RACES

2 o'clock P. M. at the Brookside track east of school house:
Race No. 1: Three-eighth mile and repeat, for purse of $50. The winner of this race is barred in No. 2.
Race No. 2: One-half mile dash; purse, $30.
Race No. 3: Quarter mile dash for saddle horses; purse, $20.
Entrance fee in above races will be ten per cent. of the purse, the same to be applied as second money, and in all races there must be three to start.

Grand Ball in the Evening Given by the Band. Tickets, $1.00.

Klamath Falls Brass Band Fourth of July Program, 1900
Klamath County Museum 1260.1981.000.0026

Evening Herald June 16, 1915 "Scattered Shots"

*"**Success to the new council**." If everybody would show the spirit that the Klamath Falls Military band did last night by boosting, instead of "crabbing," how much more pleasant things would be. There would be considerable more accomplished, at any rate.*

The Klamath Falls Military Band 1906-1922

**The Klamath Falls Military Band in Front of Baldwin Hotel, 1911
Klamath County Museum 0016.1966.066.0214**

The Klamath Falls Military Band enjoyed great community support and enthusiasm during its existence from around 1906 to 1922. The band offered a multitude of entertainment opportunities and played a crucial role in community celebrations and the economic development of the burgeoning town of Klamath Falls in the early 1900s.

The band was not connected to any branch of the armed services, but it rather used the "military band" moniker as a marker of a certain style of music. This musical style descended from military music, which initially developed as a way to enhance communication on the battlefield. Over time, the role of military bands became more ceremonial, and many community bands used the term to define themselves as a band that could play for patriotic or military events and ceremonies.

The Klamath Falls Military Band, often recognized as the premier musical organization in Southern Oregon during its time, consisted of local men who worked a wide variety of jobs but then donated their free time to band rehearsals and performances. At various times, the finances allowed for a salaried director for the band.

Though initial reviews praised the band for its excellent performances, the band still faced some initial challenges with low concert attendance and financial uncertainty. An article published in the *Klamath Republican* on May 24, 1906 reveals some of these challenges. The author urged the local community to show support for the newly organized group.

Klamath Republican May 24, 1906 "The Band Concert"

Excellent rendition of program by local talent. The concert by the Klamath Falls Military Band was given in the opera house Saturday evening, and was fairly well attended. Those who were fortunate enough to be present were greatly surprised at the work of the boys, and those who failed to attend missed a musical treat. If this organization had come here with some foreign name tacked on to them, charged three times the price asked, the opera house would have been packed. They could have dished up any kind of a tin-pan, horn blowing program and it would have been "perfectly lovely." That's because they were not home talent! But along come our boys, practice in the evening after working all day, put out a better article than the average touring organizations, and just because they are one of us, belong at home, try and keep things lively on festive occasions, there are many who "pass them up," or, if they do buy a ticket, do it as a charity. This is an injustice to the band boys. Their concert was above average, they gave the public more than it paid for, and they have good cause to feel proud of their first public appearance. Mr. Daniel has done good work, and it is to be hoped that when they again propose an entertainment they will meet with that hearty co-operation and patronage they deserve.

The Klamath Falls Military Band on Parade
Klamath County Museum 0016.1966.066.2682

The Klamath Falls Military Band in the Fourth of July Parade, 1907
Klamath County Museum 0016.1966.066.1099

The first bandleader for the Klamath Falls Military Band was a man named Ivan Daniel. Daniel played an instrumental role in garnering support for the band early on. He served as bandleader from the band's beginnings in 1906 until 1913 with a brief sabbatical from 1910-1911. During this break, Daniel was still involved in the band as a French horn player.

Ivan Daniel worked in Klamath Falls as the manager for the Klamath Falls Soda Works, a business owned by his wife's father M.W. Espy. He was also employed for the railroad (Klamath Echoes Volume 7, 1969: 75).

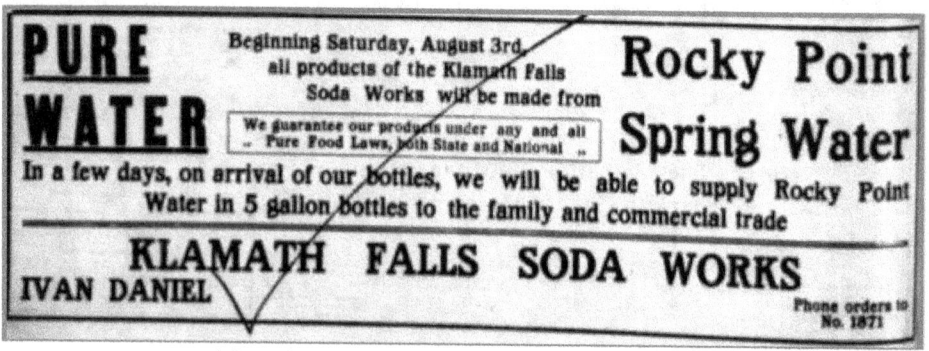

Advertisement for Klamath Falls Soda Works
Evening Herald, **August 2, 1912**

Tragedy struck the Daniel family from 1912 to 1913 with a sudden string of family member deaths. In March of 1912, Mr. Espy, the father of Daniel's wife, passed from heart disease (Evening Herald, 03-23-1912). A couple months later, the Daniel's infant son Ivan Espy Daniel died at the age of 9 months and 23 days (Evening Herald, 06-03-1912). Finally, on the Fourth of July in 1913, Ivan Daniel lost his life in the train tunnel near Dorris.

Daniel was on his way to a gig in Dorris, riding a hand cart on the railroad tracks. When Daniel entered the tunnel, a train entered on the opposite end. Daniel was unable to escape the train and lost his life. His remains are buried in the Linkville Pioneer Cemetery in Klamath Falls along with his infant son and other members of his family.

Ivan Daniel Grave Marker, Linkville Cemetery

Many people attended Daniel's funeral, and his musical friends even performed a tribute in his memory. The local newspaper reported, "One of the largest assemblages ever gathered here for such a sad mission was at the Odd Fellows hall this morning to pay its last sad respects to the remains of Ivan Daniel, who lost his life in a tunnel near Dorris on the afternoon of the Fourth" (Evening Herald, 07-08-1913).

It is suggested in the Klamath Echoes (Volume 7, 1969: 75) that a post office in the Worden area was opened in 1926 and named "Ivan" as a memorial to Ivan Daniel, though the exact location and other details are unknown.

Under the direction of Ivan Daniel, the Klamath Falls Military Band held weekly summer concerts, went on steamboat excursions on Upper Klamath Lake, and hosted dances at the band's home base in the Withrow-Melhase building and other venues.

The band's weekly concerts took place in different locations around downtown Klamath Falls. Early on, the band performed these community concerts in "court house square," a small park located in front of the courthouse in downtown Klamath Falls. Other popular venues for these weekly affairs included the Central school, skating pavilion, and various street corners and open spaces around the downtown area.

Klamath Republican February 14, 1907 "The Band"

The balmy weather that this section is now enjoying turns the thoughts toward summer and connected there with is the desire of many that band concerts be given. This question was put up to the band this week, and its members stated that they would give weekly concerts during the summer for the sum of $300, provided the city erected a band stand, whereon the concerts could be given. This is a pretty small figure being less that twenty-cents per man, and will do little more than pay for the music used in such concerts. In connection with this matter attention should be drawn to the last dance given by this organization. It resulted in the receipt of $32. This is little short of a disgrace to the city. No better band can be found on the coast.

The members have been faithful in their work, and their leader, Mr. Daniels, indefatigable in his efforts to bring the band up to its degree of perfection. This has cost the boys a good deal of money. They have in equipment and instruments over $1,100. To secure this they have raised $695, for all of which they have given their services, either in public concerts or playing at public functions. The impression seems to prevail that the band is a public property. This is wrong. It is as much a private concern as any business house in town, but is very much a part of the public enterprise and should, therefore, meet with more cordial support than has been accorded to it in the past.

**The Klamath Falls Military Band Outdoor Concert and Bandstand
Klamath County Museum 2019.050.0032**

Steamboat excursions on Upper Klamath Lake were a popular fundraiser for the group. The band would load up one of the local steamboats, typically the Winema, and set out on Upper Klamath Lake in the morning. They provided musical entertainment as the boat made its way to the Pelican Bay or Odessa area, where participants would enjoy a picnic before heading back to town (Klamath Republican, 06-21-1906).

Klamath Republican, June 21, 1906 "Music on the Water"

There will be fifty miles of good music next Sunday – band music by more than twenty pieces. Upper Klamath Lake boasts some magnificent echoes: you can hear sounds, oft repeated, flung down long canyons, to be taken up again by other natural corridors. The lake itself is a charming one. A trip to Pelican Bay Lodge is always enjoyable. The Klamath Falls Military Band is more than a collection of players. It is really a good band – an unusually good band. Two new cornet players join the band this week. The Steamer Winema is a credit to the county. Large and comfortable and sufficiently fast. Next Sunday the band gives a concert excursion to the Lodge and return on the Winema. Dinner at the Lodge. The steamer can accommodate 350 passengers. Everybody's going that can get away. Boat leaves at 8:30.

**The Steamer Winema During an Excursion on Upper Klamath Lake
Klamath County Museum 0015.1973.008.0216**

The Klamath Falls Military Band on the Steamer Winema
Klamath County Museum 0016.1966.066.2647b

The Klamath Falls Military Band at Pelican Bay or Odessa
Klamath County Museum 0015.1973.008.0279

The band also held numerous dances as a fundraiser for the group, and these took place in several popular venues around town. Many of these events took place at Houston's Opera House in downtown Klamath Falls.

Evening Herald April 18, 1912
"Band Ball will be Given Soon"

Purpose of Terpsichorean doings will be to raise wherewithal to defray cost of new togs. One week from tomorrow night the Klamath Falls Military Band will give a grand ball at the Houston opera house, which is expected to be the ne plus ultra in the terpsichorean line. The arrangement will be to have the band precede the dance with a brief concert, after which band music for dancing will ensue for an hour or so. Succeeding the band in furnishing music will be a seven-piece orchestra, which will continue to produce the necessary strains to keep the dancers keyed up until the close of the function. Admission tickets will be a dollar, each ticket to be good for a young man and his "company." The proceeds of the evening will be devoted to paying for the uniforms for the bandsmen, recently ordered.

The Withrow-Melhase Building
Klamath County Museum 2475.2008.054.0009

The band's "clubhouse" at the Withrow-Melhase building was a fundraising experiment that ultimately failed. Ivan Daniel explains the entire situation in a letter appearing in the *Evening Herald* on May 26, 1909. Daniel wrote this letter in response to some public outrage at the fact that the Klamath Falls Military Band was going to charge a fee for the band's performances on Railroad Day.

Evening Herald, May 26, 1909
"Gives the Band Side of Question"

For some time past there seems to have been gaining headway an impression to the effect that the Klamath Falls Military Band is lacking in appreciation of the favors it has been receiving at the hands of the people of Klamath Falls. This feeling has recently shown itself in expressions of amazement on the part of some of our citizens that the band should, after all it has received in donations, have the temerity to actually charge for its services on Railroad Day!

Now let us inquire into this matter and see what justification, if any, there is for such an impression. Some three years ago the band was organized "for the pleasure and musical improvement of its members and in an effort to establish a permanent musical organization which might be a credit to the town of Klamath Falls." It is strictly amateur, one of the principal clauses of the constitution stating that no member shall receive any compensation for his musical services. We were allowed to use the room over the City Hall for our rehearsals, and our only expenses consisted in music, instruments, equipment, light and fuel. During the first two years there was expended for these purposes over $1000, raised entirely by engagements of the band, excursions, dances, etc. or contributions of the individual members. During this period there was just one donation of money to the band, and that was $2 tossed into the circle while we were playing on the street near the Lakeside Inn.

When the room over City Hall was turned over to the firemen, and we were obliged to seek new quarters, the Inland Empire club graciously consented to our practicing in their club rooms, but the practicing of a brass band is hardly conducive to sweet dreams, and on account of the fact of other tenants in the building were often trying to sleep during our rehearsals, our stay there was short. We found ourselves without a home. For a while we held our meeting at the homes of the members, or gave up practicing altogether, until the idea was advanced of forming a club. Our plan was that with enough members at $1 a month to pay the running expenses of the club, the band could earn enough outside and by giving dances to add sufficiently to the income to make it considerably more desirable as a club than it could be made by the amount collected for dues alone. We had about $150 when the club was organized, which was expended for furniture, remodeling of rooms, decorations, etc. We bought a pool table and later a billiard table. We excluded non-members excepting visitors to the city, and, in fact, did everything in our *power to make the quarters comfortable and pleasant, and, as a club, worth the $1 a month the associate members paid.*

The running expenses had been as follows: rent, $30: light and water, $13: janitor, $10: fuel $3: installments on billiard table $15: piano rent $3: secretary's and collector's commission, about $5; other incidental expenses, about $4: total, $83.10. The total amount collected as club dues from the associate members has not averaged $45 a month, hence instead of the band being supported by contributions of its associate members, the band has paid out of its own earnings as a musical organization and amount equal to, if not in excess, of that paid by the associates to the support of a club which we have used but once a week as a band, and not oftener than that as individuals.

The membership was not solicited for the support of the band, nor was the members' monthly dues asked for that purpose. On the contrary, the band has always been and probably always will be absolutely self-supporting. We have never asked for a dollar from any individual nor organization as a gift, and we never will.

As an experiment, the club plan has been a disastrous failure. The band has sunk in the venture several hundred dollars, which we would otherwise now have in our treasury, and the associate members have contributed a like amount toward the maintenance of a club, which they, or part of them at least, did not attend, and of that amount the band has not used for its own purpose during the whole year more than $100. There has been absolutely no grounds for the assertion that the associate members were contributing their club dues for the benefit of the band. It was thoroughly understood when each man was asked to become a member what his dues were to be used for and what he was to get in return for them. The band asked the use of the club rooms only two nights a week, and one of those nights was for the purpose of giving a dance to raise funds for the club's benefit. The last dance we gave sent out over 200 invitations, and to associate members complimentary tickets, and fifteen people came!

Now there are two sides to every question, and for justice to be done, both sides must be heard. Perhaps you have heard the other side. I have tried to give you our side. If the fair-minded reader is still in doubt, I have failed. If convinced, say so to the Chamber of commerce committee, for we are going to disband that club and go it alone, and we need that $100. IVAN DANIEL

In addition to the various events held for the local community, the Klamath Falls Military Band also served an important role as a welcoming committee for important visitors in Klamath. The band was a marker of progress and culture, and community business leaders were eager to show off these traits to important visitors from San Francisco, Portland, and other business centers. After all, a community that could support a vibrant and high-quality band was surely an excellent place for business opportunities.

Dance and Band Concert Advertisement
Evening Herald on July 12, 1922

The leadership of the Klamath Falls Military Band became quite tumultuous starting in 1910. Numerous articles about the band mention that Ivan Daniel "left" and was no longer the band leader. W. W. Nickerson was chosen as a bandleader in February 1910. However, in 1911 William A. Snow served as bandleader (Klamath Republican, 02-10-1910; Evening Herald, 05-02-1911). Ivan Daniel was still listed as a band member playing the horn in several newspaper articles during this time, but by 1913, he was again announced as the bandleader until his untimely death later that year (Evening Herald 05-03-1911; Evening Herald, 05-13-1912).

The Klamath Falls Military Band on Main Street
Klamath County Museum 0016.1966.066.0640

The Klamath Falls Military Band Performance on Main Street
Klamath County Museum 0015.1973.008.0861

The Klamath Falls Military Band Main Street Parade
Klamath County Museum 0365.2008.001.0492

The Klamath Falls Military Band Main Street Parade
Klamath County Museum 0016.1966.066.0641

The Klamath Falls Military Band in Front of the Baldwin Hotel, 1911
Klamath County Museum 0015.1973.008.1123

The band persisted through the 1910s, though the organization of the group appears to have been undertaken more on an annual basis after the passing of Ivan Daniel in 1913. The first bit of activity for the band after Daniel's passing in July of 1913 occurred the next month. Klamath's Chamber of Commerce proposed sending the band, under the direction of a Mr. Robert A. Mitchell, on an auto tour through Central Oregon to the Pendleton Round-Up. The trip was seen as an advertising opportunity for the city of Klamath Falls (Evening Herald, 08-26-1913).

Evening Herald August 26, 1913
"Bandsmen's Tour Appears Certain"

Chamber of Commerce has offered its help, and business men volunteer to assist in the matter. The proposed automobile trip of the Klamath Falls Military Band through Central Oregon to the Pendleton Round-Up, and return via Eugene and the Rogue River Valley, today appears to be a certainty, so quickly has the public volunteered to assist the musicians. Realizing the immense advertising value of the trip, the Klamath Chamber of Commerce this morning informed Director Mitchell of the band that the organization would be glad to assist the band in securing funds. Business men have also made voluntary offers. The plans at present are for the band to leave early next month in automobiles, visiting Lakeview, Burns, Bend, Prineville, Pendleton, The Dalles and Eugene, and on the return trip, visit the cities in the Rogue River Valley. At each place, they will give concerts and a dance to help defray their expenses. Nearly all of the bandsmen today stated that they would be able to go with the party. The band is considering giving a dance or two before leaving here, as a means of swelling the exchequer.

The community continuously celebrated the Klamath Falls Military Band for its quality performances. This is most evident in the numerous articles appearing in the local newspaper announcing that the band would be receiving money from the city of Klamath Falls for its services in weekly summer concerts. At times, there was much controversy surrounding the amount of money requested by the band (Evening Herald, 05-05-1915; Evening Herald, 05-18-1915). However, community leaders generally saw the band as a great advertisement for the community and considered the money an investment in the economic development of the region. The news that Klamath Falls would pay up to $300 for the organization of a community band throughout the summer was apparently big news, as newspapers as far away as Oakland, California reported about the decision (Oakland Tribune, 05-23-1915). It may not sound like a lot today. However, according to the Bureau of Labor Statistics, $300 in 1915 had as much spending power as about $7500 in today's money (Bureau of Labor Statistics Inflation Calculator).

Evening Herald May 5, 1915
"Money Voted for Band Then is Reconsidered"

For several minutes last night, the Klamath Falls Band, now in course of organization, basked in the wealth of a real income of $75 per month. But only for a few minutes. On behalf of the musicians, E.R. Willis appeared before the council and asked for an appropriation of $75 a month, to be used toward paying the salary of a capable leader for the organization. In return, it was stated by Willis, the band will render weekly concerts during June, July, August, and September, the months during which the $75 a month was to be paid by the city. After some discussion, Councilman Hamilton moved that the appropriation be made for the four months. This carried with Matthews, Hamilton and Lockwood voting yes and Rogers and Owens no. The vote did not settle the discussion, however. After this was taken, there was talk about the advisability of having the appropriation made through the passage of an ordinance to that effect. As a result of this, Lockwood moved for a reconsideration. This was voted and the appropriation is just where it was before it was voted upon. There is much disappointment among the bandmen at the failure to secure the appropriation last night, as this delays somewhat the securing of a director. However, the musicians are of the opinion that the councilmen are in favor of a series of weekly concerts by a good band, and hope to see the ordinance introduced. "I am willing to give $10 a month through the bank for the maintenance of the band, but I hesitate about spending the city's money in this way," said Councilmen Rogers, "especially after the defeat of the charter amendment for increased pay for the city engineer. I think the band asks for too much money, and believe that $25 a month would be nearer right." The discussion preceding the reconsideration was brought about by Mayor Nicholas, who cited the charter provision that money in excess of $100 cannot be appropriated without ordinance.

Evening Herald May 18, 1915
"Council Votes Money for Band"

The council last night passed the ordinance appropriating $75 a month during June, July, August, and September for the maintenance of the Klamath Falls Military band. It is now up to Mayor Nicholas for approval. In return for the money appropriated by the city, the band is to render one concert a week during the summer season, these concerts to be held in the court house square, central school grounds, or some other public place.

Oakland Tribune May 23, 1915
"City Pays for Music"

Klamath Falls, May 22 – The Klamath Falls city council has passed an ordinance appropriating $75 a month during June, July, August, and September for the maintenance of the Klamath Falls Military band. In return for the money appropriated by the city the band will give one concert a week during the summer season at the court house park.

The Military Band (Center) at the Arrival of the First Train, 1909
Klamath County Museum 2486.2012.017.0227

With financial support from the city of Klamath Falls, the band was able to secure salaried band leaders, raising the professionalism and visibility of the band to an even higher level. In 1915, the band recruited a band leader all the way from Los Angeles named A.C. Schloss (Evening Herald 06-05-1915).

Evening Herald June 5, 1915
"New Band Leader is Here for Job"

A.C. Schloss comes in from Los Angeles highly recommended – initial practice tomorrow. Klamath Falls' Military band now has a salaried leader. This is A.C. Schloss, who arrived last night from Los Angeles, to take up the direction of the local organization. The first rehearsal will be held by Mr. Schloss at 2:30 tomorrow at the Pavilion, and all musicians are asked to attend. A series of concerts is to be given weekly in the court house square, and the new director wishes to know what instruments are needed, that he may send for outside musicians to come here for the summer.

Unfortunately, the draw of a salaried band leader position was not enough to maintain stable leadership for the band. A.C. Schloss did not last very long and was soon replaced by H. H. Howell of Medford. The band still saw increased opportunities to perform, even becoming the "house band" for local baseball games (Evening Herald, 06-23-1915). They also played for important local ceremonies including the opening of the new road on Upper Klamath Lake, "Klamath's Appian Way," which was an important route to the north of Klamath before the creation of Highway 97 (Evening Herald, 08-23-1915).

Evening Herald June 23, 1915
"Band and Ball Team Give Ball"

Two organizations combine for big public ball to be given Wednesday night in the Pavilion. The Klamath Falls ball team and the Klamath Falls Military band have combined forces, and will give a big municipal ball team and band benefit ball in the Pavilion next Wednesday night. The band will furnish the music and the members of the ball team will furnish the ladies – at least that is the way the players- ball players-state it. The band needs the money for equipment, and so does the ball team. H.H. Howell of Medford, formerly with the Andrews opera company, which visited this city recently, and who also put on a cantata for the Elks here two years ago, will arrive in the city Saturday night to take charge of the local band. His intentions at present are to remain here if the situation looks favorable. The band will give its weekly concert on the lawn of the Central School building tonight at 7 o'clock.

Evening Herald August 23, 1915
"Falls Band Will Go Tomorrow"

Will accompany road boosters to opening of new road along the Upper Klamath Lake tomorrow night. The Klamath Falls Military band will make the trip with the road boosters, who will formally open the new $70,000 road on Upper Klamath Lake, called "Klamath's Appian Way," tomorrow night. The road was opened yesterday, but has not been officially accepted by the county court as yet. Judge Hanks will inspect it after his return from San Francisco. The Commercial Club is boosting the opening of the road, and desires all possible to go.

Despite the general approval and support surrounding the Klamath Falls Military Band at this time, the band all but folded temporarily in 1916. A small group still performed for some baseball games and other small events, but there was no official organized band during this year (Evening Herald, 06-07-1916; Evening Herald, 03-01-1917).

The absence of an organized band was felt in the community. A local business leader, Robert Strahorn, even offered to furnish uniforms for a new band to help spur the reorganization of the band (Evening Herald, 11-13-1916).

Evening Herald November 13, 1916
"Strahorn will help new band"

Railroad builder offers to furnish uniforms for an up-to-date band for Klamath Falls. An offer from Robert E. Strahorn to furnish uniforms has started a movement for an up-to-date band for Klamath Falls. Already there are several good players in town and others could be induced to come from the outside if the band is given proper support. Most of the players have their own instruments, and with new uniforms furnished by Mr. Strahorn a good band seems assured. The need of a band in Klamath Falls is considered apparent. On many such occasions as those of the past week – the auto parade Friday afternoon and Community Day – a band was almost indispensable.

Local musicians themselves were desperate to organize the band after an inactive year. In May 1917, it was announced that a bandleader, W.H. McLaughlin, had been secured (Evening Herald, 05-12-1917). The band was still seen as an excellent opportunity to advertise and show-off the local community. This time, an idea was floated that the band could be supported by a "subscription list" of local businesses pledging support for the organization rather than a sole payment from the city (Evening Herald 05-22-1917).

> ## *Evening Herald May 12, 1917 "Plans Are for Band Here"*
>
> *Local bandmen have organized and a leader has been secured – bandmen believe good opportunity here. Klamath Falls shall have a band is the intention of the band men of the city. At a meeting which was recently held, every bandman agreed to heartily support an organization and to donate his services toward advancement of an organization which is lacking in Klamath Falls. W.H. McLaughlin, a thoroughly competent musician, has already been chosen as bandmaster of the prospective organization, and through his leadership and sound support, we will be assured of one of the best musical organizations in the state, say bandmen. There is much good talent here, which has been idle, owing to lack of interest and leaders. There are several good openings here for capable musicians, and the new organization is already in touch with men who ... The bandmen have already pledged their support. "It takes more – it calls for the support of the city, of the business...In the past few months there has been evidence of a ...where a band was wanted, where a band was really needed. Whenever possible the boys have ...a scattering few, and did their best to cope with the situation. They have been heartily applauded for their efforts. It would be a great credit to the city, a good advertisement...*

The year of 1917 shaped up to be quite busy for the Klamath Falls Military Band. They played for baseball games, held their weekly concerts, and played for numerous engagements around town (Evening Herald, 06-29-1917; Evening Herald, 06-19-1917). It is worth mentioning that 1917 was the last year that the "Klamath Falls Military Band" moniker was used. Moving forward, articles refer to the "Klamath Falls band," or the "Klamath Falls Brass Band" instead. (Evening Herald, 06-20-1917; Evening Herald, 06-21-1917).

Evening Herald May 22, 1917
"City Band Makes Rapid Progress"

Eighteen men attended rehearsal last night. Plans being laid for a concert early in June. Eighteen men were in the line-up for last night's rehearsal of the city band which is making rapid progress and is getting into shape for its first public appearance. Several new men are expected to arrive in the city within the next few weeks to increase the size and the strength of the organization. The Klamath Falls Businessmen's Association has voted to assist in financing the band through a subscription list, according to band men, and other business firms of the city are to be asked for a small monthly subscription. Local band men have been working several weeks now on organizing, securing a competent leader and arranging all details. Many occasions for the use of a band are already looming up for the summer and fall season and the band men who have loyally turned out this spring several times, believe Klamath should have an organization of which the city will be proud. The band plans to give its first concert during the first week in June.

Evening Herald June 20, 1917
"Klamath Band Concert Tonight"

First public concert to be given on Central School Plaza – Eight Players Coming for July 3-4 Celebration. The Klamath Falls Military band will appear in its first concert tonight at 7:30 o'clock sharp at the Central school building plaza, at the corner of Tenth and Main streets. This will be the first public concert given by the band this summer. The city council took steps Monday night to pay the band the sum of $250 for a period of five months of concerts. It was announced today that arrangements have been completed for the securing of eight additional players to put the band in the best of shape for the July 3-4 celebration, which will give the organization an instrumentation of twenty-five pieces. Director Wm. H. McLaughlin has been working hard to put the men in shape for the season, and several past appearances have been a credit to his ability as a director and leader and to the personnel of the organization. The program for tonight is as follows: [program included].

Evening Herald June 28, 1918 "Notice"

All members of the Klamath Falls band will meet at the Elks temple promptly at 7:45 this evening and march in a body to the War Stamp mass meeting on Klamath avenue.

Evening Herald June 21, 1917
"Band Concert Much Enjoyed by Audience"

The band concert given last night by the Klamath Falls Military Band was much enjoyed by the large audience that attended. The work of the band is exceptional and a number of the selections last night are not ordinarily played by a more or less volunteer and unpaid organization, as Klamath Falls has.

In 1918, the Klamath Falls Band developed a close relationship with the local Elks Temple, holding rehearsals and performances at the temple and participating in several Elks events (Evening Herald, 06-11-1918; Evening Herald, 06-12-1918). With the climax of World War I taking place at this time, many of these events were geared towards support of the war effort (Evening Herald, 06-29-1918; Evening Herald, 06-28-1918; Evening Herald, 09-20-1918).

Evening Herald June 28, 1918
"Monster War Stamp Meetings Tonight"

Huge gathering in city will be held on Klamath Avenue. Band Music and Splendid Talks. Other Meetings in School house in all sections of the county...While the program arranged is very short, it is going to be unusually fine. The Klamath Falls Brass Band will play inspiring marches and brief addresses will be made regarding the "Baby Bonds" and what their sale means toward carrying the war to successful issue.

Evening Herald September 20, 1918
"War Train Will Visit this City Sunday"

...Arrangements to have the Klamath Falls band on hand have been made and there will be other varieties of patriotic demonstrations by the citizens here...

The band also had a new leader once again. This time a former band member who ended up in New York came back to Klamath Falls to serve as bandleader for the summer of 1918 (Evening Herald, 07-09-1918).

Close Up on the Military Band in Front of the Baldwin Hotel
Klamath County Museum 2486.2008.070.0055

The Klamath Falls Military Band in Front of the Baldwin Hotel
Klamath County Museum 0365.2008.001.0490.2

The Klamath Falls Military Band on Parade
Klamath County Museum 2019.003.0007

The Klamath Falls Military Band on Parade
Klamath County Museum 2486.2012.017.0827

Evening Herald July 9, 1918
"New Leader is Here For Brass Band"

First practice will be held at Elks Temple tonight – Leader Arrives From New York – Former Resident. The first band practice by the Klamath Falls band will be held this evening at the Elks temple, at 3 o'clock, under the leadership of James Newnham, who has recently arrived from New York to take charge of the local organization. Mr. Newnham was here and played in the local band six or seven years ago and is well known by many of the players. With the fine talent demonstrated by the home boys on many occasions there is no doubt but that a fine band can be developed under an experienced leader.

The organization of the band continued to be difficult from year to year. Only one newspaper article appears in the year 1920. The article mentions a newly arrived community member named R.H. Wonderly, who wanted to serve as bandleader. The band was again seeking financial support to cover the costs for weekly concerts through the summer. Given that no other articles have been found about band activity during this year, it is probably safe to say that they were not very successful in this endeavor (Evening Herald, 05-15-1920).

Evening Herald May 15, 1920 "Prospects for a City Band"

The question of organization of a band was brought up last evening at the meeting at the city hall. R.H. Wonderly, newly arrived here, stated that he had considerable experience as a band instructor. He said that he had talked with local people and found plenty of material here for a good band and an active sentiment in favor of organization. The cost, he said, for one street concert a week during the summer would probably be $300 a month. He offered to donate his services as instructor. This would pay for a band of from 20 to 25 pieces, he said. At the close of discussion Mr. Wonderly and Earl Shepherd were appointed a committee to canvass the city and find out if general sentiment approved the band and would support it financially to the extent of $250 or $300 a month.

The band once again faced financial uncertainty in 1921. This time, there was much controversy surrounding the exit of director Fred Seelak as seen in an article that appeared in the Evening Herald at the end of the summer band season (Evening Herald, 09-15-1921; Evening Herald, 10-07-1921).

Evening Herald October 7, 1921
"With Director Gone Band is Likely to Quit"

Klamath Falls is without a band leader, and the musical organization built up this summer under the direction of Fred Seelak will probably dissolve, according to members of the musical organization. A.L. Wishard, manager of the band, told the story of the trials and tribulations of the capable leader who left here last week for a California point. "Seelak has left us just at the time when the finest musical organization which this city has ever known was reaching the perfection point. But don't be hasty and blame him. He was justified in departing. Any man who exerted the best there was in him to build up the kind of band he did, use his own money to buy music with, deprive his family of personal necessities to keep his word with the band boys, battle for a living in a community which failed to recognize his worth, and then have the fruits of his all-summer work passed up by all save a few – Well, that would take the heart out of an optimist." Seelak was recently promised $100 by the chamber of commerce, and a committee appointed to solicit the money. Band members said Seelak did not receive the money, and A.J. Voye, chairman of the solicitation committee, bore out the statement. Seelak claimed the chamber was responsible for his coming here, promising him financial assistance, but when he tried to collect he was continually put off. When his house rent fell due he was unable to meet it. Band members thought Seelak a good leader and express unanimous regret over his leaving. Secretary Stanley was asked some time ago if the chamber was responsible for Director Seelak locating here, but denied the responsibility, saying that he came here of his own accord. Chairman Voye of the soliciting committee told a Herald representative this afternoon over the telephone that the money was never solicited, never turned over to the chamber nor paid to the band director, to his knowledge. Some criticism was made this week because the band was supposed to lead the parade at the opening of the fair Wednesday, but no parade, band, or even the semblance of a parade showed at the appointed time. Charges were made that the band refused to parade Wednesday because the Fourth of July committee never paid them the $600 due them. Treasurer Furber of the Fourth committee has denied the charge made by producing the cancelled checks to the bandmen, and states that the story is a fabrication. A.L. Wishard, manager of the band, also denies the charge, as he was present when the money was paid over to the band

The Klamath Falls Military Band would come full circle in 1922 when band members once again recruited W.A. Snow, who had previously directed the band, to return as bandleader after another potential bandleader, J.O. Fritz, left town (Evening Herald, 06-26-1922). Under the direction of Snow, the band returned to some of its early practices, such as holding dances for fundraisers (Evening Herald, 07-06-1922). This time, some major businesses also kicked in some support, including Klamath Lumber and Box and Big Lakes (Evening Herald, 07-12-1922). These companies specifically mentioned the community benefits of the band, citing the number of different types of workers, professionals, and tradesmen that might be drawn to the community because of its high-quality band and the opportunity to play in the community organization.

Evening Herald July 6, 1922
"City Offered Opportunity for Good Band"

18 trained musicians are available; W.A. Snow Secured as Leader. Opportunity for a band organization that will be a credit to this community, and unsurpassed by any similar organizations on the coast, is offered Klamath Falls this summer. Eighteen trained bandsmen are available and the chamber of commerce committee handling the matter – A.L. Wishard, J.J. Furber, and J.A. Gordon – have secured W.A. Snow, who directed the local band in 1910 and 1911 and made it the best band organization the city has ever had, as a leader. A plan for financing the band that will give all an opportunity to contribute has been worked out in a series of dances at the open-air pavilion, the first one Thursday evening July 13. Tickets will sell at one dollar each. A concert will precede the dance and dances and concerts will be held during July, August, and September. It is hoped that sufficient funds can be raised in this way to carry the band along until other means of financing it can be worked out. The success of the band depends upon the amount of support that is generally given. The band members are devoting much time to practice and are willing to continue to devote their time without compensation. The committee is now seeking for a corps of ladies who can spare the time to sell tickets for the first dance, and ask all volunteers to report to the secretary at the chamber of commerce rooms. Since this is strictly a community affair, said the committee chairman, we feel that everyone in the community will want to contribute a share. Consequently, we decided this means of raising a fund would be better than the circulation of a subscription list among the business men. This does not mean that the business men will be excluded, for each can purchase as many tickets as he wishes and this applies to all other citizens. As a matter of fact, the business men realize the benefits of band and will support it liberally. The band will do their part to make the organization a success and we hope all citizens will reciprocate. The band will give an open-air concert once a week, and on patriotic holidays and special occasions when a band is needed they will be ready and willing to furnish music. The chamber of commerce, city officials and civic organizations generally are strongly supporting the proposal for a permanent band organization. The permanency is assured through the permanent residence here of 15 of the present band members. Tickets for the first dance will be ready Saturday morning, and if they find a ready sale the success of the movement will be virtually assured.

Evening Herald July 12, 1922
"Band Movement is Given Help by Box Plants"

Klamath Lumber and Box and Big Lakes Pledge Aid; Others Volunteer. If everybody rallies to the band support as strongly as the box factories are coming in, there is no doubt that Klamath Falls will have a band this summer. G.A. Krause of the Klamath Lumber and Box company started the box factory contributions by volunteering to take a dollar ticket for each of the factory employees to Thursday evening's dance and concert. M.S. West pledged the Big Lakes Box company would fall into line and other plants are expected to follow their example, according to A.L. Wishard, chairman of the chamber of commerce band committee. Mrs. A.F. Glover, working single-handed, sold over $50 worth of tickets up to today. This is encouraging, said Wishard, and the support of those who have sensed the importance of the movement is highly appreciated. But the campaign needs more general support to make it the success it should be. If the attempt to maintain a band fails this time, it will probably be years before it can be revived and therefore it is urged that everybody get in and help; not leaving the success or failure of the band in the hands of a few extra willing workers. As the band idea becomes more familiar to the public, enthusiasm develops rapidly in proportion as the benefits become apparent. In looking about for musicians to increase the band membership, Chairman Wishard has discovered an amazing amount of interest in Klamath Falls. He has saved only the most promising answers and has a stack of letters several inches high from musicians who want to locate here if the band is started. They are men of all professions and trades from banker to laborer, mostly family men of the permanent citizen class, any of whom would be a distinct asset to the community. If even one of these families would locate here permanently it would more than compensate for the season's cost of maintain a band, Wishard points out. Add the enlivening influence of a weekly band concert on the business district; the pleasure derived by the crowd and the publicity that the city will get from a class A band and the argument in its favor is overwhelming, declare its supporters. The members of the band, 14 of whom are permanent resident, ask no compensation for their services while playing for the public concerts and on general occasions, and the total cost is estimated at $150 a month for the summer season to pay the director and provide music and incidentals.

The Klamath Falls Military Band
Klamath County Museum 2486.2009.048.0214

The Klamath Falls Military Band was always seen as a credit to the town of Klamath Falls. The band took on more than just a ceremonial role, and it was actually used at times as a method of community advertising and economic development. Everyone agreed that the band was of superior quality. However, it seems not many could agree on how to finance the band's activities. After nearly a decade of tumultuous and unstable leadership and ad hoc organization from year to year, the Klamath Falls Military Band moniker was abandoned all together. Local musicians would still band together for annual performances, but the official organization of the Klamath Falls Military Band would come to an end around 1922, about sixteen years after it first was first organized. In 1923, local musicians would try a new name: The Klamath Falls Municipal Band, starting under the direction of a Mr. Cramer (Evening Herald, 01-17-1923).

Evening Herald July 11, 1918
U.S. Melodies Antidote for Pro-Germanism

President of State Music Association Delivered Inspiring Address on Subject of American Music

Keeping Pro-Germanism out of the public schools by putting American music in was urged here today by Mrs. Abbie Norton Jamieson, president of the California State Music Teacher's organization's four-day annual convention.

"Only the most loyal and inspiring American music should be taught the boys and girls of the state's educational institutions," Mrs. Jamieson said. "If there are any text books in use that contain German songs, those compositions should be removed."

Loyalty was the outstanding feature of the meeting. The music at a concert under the auspices of the organization was strictly and patriotically American in both its immediate and its ultimate purpose, as the proceeds were to be devoted to the purchase of bonds of the Fourth Liberty Loan to be floated next fall. Other concerts for the same purpose are scheduled for later convention days.

Praise for young musicians who have joined the colors was generously given and the declaration was made that the musical standard of the United States Army was at least the equal of that of any other fighting force.

The increase in the numerical strength of military bands was to be discussed.

Mrs. Jamieson said the federal government approved the holding of the convention, press sanction having been obtained from William G. McAdoo, secretary of the treasury, because some member questioned the propriety of the gathering on account of the expense incurred

The Klamath Falls Municipal Band

Though by most accounts the municipal band was simply a continuation of the Klamath Falls Military Band, the first use of this band name in 1923 marked an effort to create a new, permanent organization, rather than the ad hoc organization of a band from year to year that had taken place for nearly a decade (Evening Herald, 01-17-1923).

Evening Herald January 17, 1923
"Municipal Band Issues Plea For Support Of City"

Efforts being made to give public first-class organization; funds are needed. At 1 o'clock tomorrow afternoon the band will parade on Main Street to give the public an idea of what it can do, it was announced this afternoon. A plea for support by citizens of this city of the Klamath Falls Municipal band by better attendance at entertainments staged by the band, was contained in a statement issued today by the board of managers of the band. The plea cites the struggles for existence the band organization has undergone during the past year, pointing out that at present prospects are bright for a high-class, permanent band with a competent leader, and that the good-will of the general public is both needed and merited. The statement follows: To the citizens of Klamath Falls: You may have noticed last week of the organization of the Klamath Falls Municipal Band. This is the first time in the past 10 years that we have been able to get right down to business and effect a real organization. In 1910 and 1911 we had a first-class organization. You who were here this year will recall that we gave concerts every week, and on numerous special occasions. We would like to do the same this year and, in the years, to come. Last year we made an attempt and did the best we could but our chief difficulty was in not being able to get a good leader. This year we have overcome this difficulty by having *secured a first-class leader, Mr. Cramer, who, we have every reason to believe, will stay with us. Mr. Cramer and his family of five (all being musicians) located here last fall. They are doing well and claim that Klamath Falls is to be their home from now on. With a man of Mr. Cramer's type as leader and the members that we now have, we will be able to give Klamath Falls a real band, provided the citizens of this city will do their part. We feel that when we donate our service in rehearsing, giving weekly concerts and playing for special occasions such as Decoration Day, Armistice Day, etc., that we are doing our part. Stop and consider that we are devoting considerable time for your pleasure, therefore when you are asked to buy a ticket for a band dance, do so. This is our means of obtaining the funds necessary to keep the organization going. Last year we received $409 which is less than 10 cents per person, assuming our population to be 5,000. However, practically this entire sum was received from the merchants and the lumber companies. The merchants, the Elks lodge, the professional men, the lumber companies, and the newspaper have always helped the band. And since the band is for the benefit of the entire community, we feel that every citizen should contribute to its support. Suppose that one-half of the citizens of this community would donate $1.00 each, then we could maintain a real band. We are giving a band dance on Friday night, January 19 at the Scandinavian hall. Do your part, buy a ticket and come to the dance. (Signed) Board of Managers, Klamath Falls Municipal Band.*

Unfortunately, it appears that the only substantial change to the band at this time was the name. Questions of finance and leadership would continue to be a problem for the band, and the organization of the group would continue to be an annual consideration.

The municipal band continued the tradition of dance fundraisers and weekly summer concerts, most of which were held either at the Elks Temple or on the lawn of the Central School (Evening Herald, 06-20-1923). In 1923, they made a point of publicizing that they would not be soliciting funds from the general public that year, but instead they had received support from local lumbermen (Evening Herald, 06-12-1923).

After rebranding as a "municipal band," the group was now on call for many other local activities. One of these was the local rodeo, which even saw the band dressing in rodeo attire at times (Evening Herald, 07-03-1923; Evening Herald, 07-01-1924). The support from local lumbermen also brought about special concerts for the benefit of lumber workers (Evening Herald, 07-24-1923)

Evening Herald July 24, 1923
"Band Concert to Be Held Wednesday at Pelican City"

Lumber workers to have opportunity to enjoy musical entertainment by city band. The municipal band concert will be held Wednesday evening at Pelican City, for the benefit of lumber workers, instead of on the Central School grounds, it was announced today by W.F. Cramer, conductor. The concert will start at 7:30.

In addition to the traditional band activities, the municipal band also participated in parades and held performances for Memorial Day and Independence Day (Klamath News, 05-20-1924; Evening Herald, 07-01-1924). They would also experiment with a Christmas concert, which was held in 1923 along with other local musical groups (Klamath News, 11-30-1923). These newer activities would become a standard for many years afterwards.

From 1923 to 1924, the municipal band enjoyed a relative stability that had not been seen since the earlier days of the Klamath Falls Military Band. However, it appears that Cramer only lasted as band leader for two years. There is no mention of him after these years, and the next mention of the band occurs in the *Klamath News* in 1926, which states that a "new band" would be making its debut by performing for the opening of the baseball season (Klamath News, 05-11-1926).

Surprisingly, Fred Selak, the very same conductor who left over controversy around funding for the Klamath Falls Military Band in 1921, reappears as the director for the municipal band in 1926 (Klamath News, 05-25-1926). An article the next month would appeal for financial support for the renewed band effort (Evening Herald, 06-16-1926; Klamath News, 06-18-1926).

Evening Herald June 16, 1926 "Let Us Have a Band"

A committee of business men will start a drive tomorrow to raise $1000 for the support of the band. The only criticism we have to offer is that it should be for at least twice that sum, but since it is their belief, and the belief of the members of the band, that $1000 will be sufficient, let us get back of the movement and put it over with a bang. Klamath Falls needs the band. It has always been somewhat of a

> *mystery to us why men will devote evening after evening to practice, set out and tramp the streets and give of their time and talent on many occasions when there is no recompense, not even appreciation. The public will turn out and listen, sometimes applaud, then turn away and forget, never asking how the band is supported. To date not one penny has been contributed for the band, and the time is at hand when this condition must be changed. The members of the band are indebted for something like $700 for uniforms. They have spent this own money for music and they have given liberally of their time in practice. We do not believe that anyone in the city will be less generous than are the band boys, and that is why we are today bringing to your attention their needs. We believe that to place it before you will be sufficient and we believe that when the men who have undertaken the task of raising funds needed get through, they will have secured more than the amount required. There are times when the people of the city will rise to an occasion, and we believe this is one of those times. Let us establish a roll of honor and on that roll let there not be a name missing. Daily we shall carry upon the front page of the Evening Herald the names of men who have contributed. They will be published not that such a procedure is desired by them, but because we want to justify our belief in the people of Klamath Falls - a belief that they do not have to be urged to do a plain duty and that they are always ready to stand for those things which will help make this city a more pleasant place in which to live.*

There was a spirited response from the community to support the local band. The Chamber of Commerce announced it had formed a committee to gain support and a number of local citizens and businesses contributed funds to the band (Klamath News, 06-16-1926; Evening Herald, 06-17-1926). The band drive was successful in raising the needed funds. Fred Seelak commented that "Klamath Falls residents may rest assured that they will have a Municipal band that will be a credit to this community…I appreciate the response of the citizens of this city in subscribing so liberally for the band in the drive that is now being prosecuted to secure a fund of $1000, and I feel sure every member of the organization feels the same as I do. For 30 years I have given my very best to have this city favored with a Municipal band, and the generosity of our people on this occasion will not be found to have been misplaced confidence" (Klamath News, 06-19-1926).

This drive for community support captured the attention of people from all walks of life. Some of them put their commentary on the subject in the local newspaper, making passionate pleas for the support of local music.

One example comes from S.E. Icenbice, who argued that the support of a local band could help build relationships between the business men of Klamath Falls and the ranchers and farmers out in the country (Evening Herald, 06-22-1926).

Evening Herald June 22, 1926
"Rancher Tells What City Band Means for All"

S.E. Icenbice believes that organization will bring many to hear concerts. "Here is two dollars and fifty cents for the band fund. If you need more let me know. If Klamath Falls can't support a band, tell us farmers so, and maybe we can help you out." Thus did S.E. Icenbice preface his remarks in the office of the The Evening Herald this morning. Continuing, he said: "Do you know why I want to see a band permanently established in Klamath Falls? Well, it is because it reminds me of my younger days. Back in Iowa and Kansas and again in Indiana, all of the towns boasted a band. And they were good bands, too. It was the custom in those days for the band to play Saturday evenings and we farmer boys and girls would hitch up the buggy and drive into town and enjoy the music. We returned to our homes happier and healthier for the recreation. I have been in Klamath county for over nineteen years and during every one of those years I have longed for a return of the Saturday evening band concerts that I so much enjoyed in my youth. If I were suggesting to the business men of Klamath Falls something that would build up a closer friendship between the city and the country, I would suggest Saturday evening band concerts. Put the band on a truck and let them play at different points in the business district and then watch the people from the country drive in and enjoy the music between the times spent in shopping in the various stores. They will return home, as we used to return to our farms back in the middle west, with a warmer glow in their hearts and a feeling that the business men of Klamath Falls are pretty good sports after all. It will gradually wean them away from the habit of spending their money out of the county and bring them to the realization that those who enjoy the music should help pay the fiddler."

The band was successful in pulling support from a wide cross section of the community. Concerts were well attended and the band received rave reviews in the newspapers for the rest of the 1926 season.

Klamath News July 17, 1926
"Vast Audience is Happy When Band Concert is Given"

An attentive audience of approximately 2000 people lined the lawns of the Central school and rested in rows of cars parked along nearby streets last evening when the municipal band, under the capable leadership of Fred Selak, played to perfection the second open-air concert of the season. Twenty of the 25 musicians comprising the band, were out in full uniform and gave an enjoyable program of lively marches, fox trots, and overtures. The crowd exceeded that of the previous concert by several hundred, in the opinion of bandsmen, and contained a great many people from outlying communities. Local music lovers are beginning to look forward to these musical treats and if the crowds continue to grow, Director Selak and his trained musicians may play to a schoolyard of folks before the summer is over.

Klamath News July 25, 1926 "To Be Proud Of"

One of the finest compliments any city can have is the ownership of a good band. Thanks to the support and encouragement of many citizens Klamath is now in line with the best of them, with fully equipped and properly uniformed band musicians who live with their program with all the soul they possess. The appearance they make and the music they play will be a proud boast from now on, and something that will add to the satisfaction of living here.

The band attempted to keep up the momentum of support into the next year. They continued to hold dance fundraisers and appeal to the local community to support the band (Evening Herald, 08-06-1926; Klamath News, 08-07-1926). Their efforts were successful as the band swelled in size to around 50 musicians and made plans for the next season as early as February in 1927 (Evening Herald, 02-01-1927).

Evening Herald February 1, 1927 "Municipal Music"

It is nearing the time when we begin to consider the springtime and summer in Klamath; when we think of the people who will enjoy the evenings down town with a band concert in progress. In order to have band concerts we must necessarily have a band we must support it. An organization of nearly fifty men now constitutes the Klamath Falls band and it is a going concern. But it needs encouragements; it needs your support. Director Selak is laying plans for the coming season, even to the extent of possibly taking his band to Salem for the state fair engagement. Open air concerts will start, we are told, as soon as the weather softens and spring comes, all of which means the band is to be a very strong part of municipal life this year. In a great many communities, a band is supported by taxation, the general public carrying the load needed to properly support a musical organization. As yet we have not reached that point here and the support is entirely voluntary. The Herald is for the band. We don't believe a city can get along without one. In order to have it, let us all get in behind a movement to give it proper support.

In 1928, the band would once again have a new director, E.D. Swinney (Evening Herald, 03-14-1928). Band activities for the year included a Memorial Day performance and a special appearance at the Lakeview Round-up rodeo and Railroad Jubilee (Klamath News, 08-26-1928). Despite the increasing activity and support from previous years, the band would once again be without a leader, until it was announced the following year that Vivian Puckett would assume leadership. However, this organization mainly appeared as an ad hoc organization for some special events that year (Klamath News, 07-02-1929).

"Pick-up" bands performed for a variety of community events from 1929 through 1930. The lack of an organized community band was enough for the paper to ask, "Why not a band?" in an editorial appearing in the *Evening Herald* on March 18, 1930. The article suggested a local organization could take charge of a local band.

The call for a city band would be answered the following year when the organization would be reorganized once again under the leadership of Fred Selak (Evening Herald, 02-11-1931; Klamath News, 02-14-1931).

Evening Herald March 18, 1930 "Why Not a Band?"

Klamath Falls is one of the few towns of any importance in the state without a band - an adult organization. This conditions not due to lack of band musicians, for a count would doubtless reveal half a hundred or more men who have had sufficient experience tooting a horn or beating a drum to qualify them for membership in a community organization. In most communities one or more lodges or civic groups sponsor the local band. Oftentimes the musicians can be controlled in this manner when, if left to themselves, they may not work together for long. The Elks or some other strong order of the city could sponsor a band to furnish music for various activities during the summer and the main expense would be for music and the services of a competent director. This suggestion is offered in view of the fact that summer finds the main body of the high school band disorganized. Graduation, summer jobs and other forces combine to disrupt the organization and it would be easier to pull together a group of older and more experienced musicians in a short space of time. It would not be a bad idea for representatives of one or more of the lodges and civic bodies to give this matter a thought and take a count of available band musicians in the city who would be willing to devote a little of their time to practice and playing weekly concerts. It is done in towns much smaller that Klamath Falls - why not here?

Evening Herald February 10, 1931
"Support the Municipal Band"

The plan to reorganize the Klamath municipal band and to stage concerts during the summer is one demanding the support of every business and professional man, and of every resident of the city. There is no community institution or organization that contributes so much to the happiness and life of the people of any town or city as a good band. There is no other organization which can give to its home community more favorable advertising then a good band, and none which can contribute more to the community spirit. There is nothing which stirs the spirit and patriotism of an individual more than the strains of a good march played by a band. There is nothing as soothing and restful as the strains of a smoothly flowing waltz when it comes from a well-directed band on a summer evening in the park. There is nothing that sets the feet a tingling more than a good Spanish dance like La Paloma and some of the old standard selections. The town or city without a good band is lacking in organization that is essential to well-rounded lives and a maximum of pleasure. Let everybody get in line and accord support to the movement now underway to reorganize and maintain the municipal band, which will contribute much to the splendid spirit pervading Klamath Falls.

Klamath News February 11, 1931
"Municipal band plans made for coming summer"

Plans initiated by local civic organizations, service clubs and businessman are underway for the reorganization of the municipal band and a series of outdoor concerts during the summer months. A program of financing the organization is now underway and is said to be a long line which will not require individual donations. As soon as the financial program is completed band men will be called together and permanent organization affected. Prof. Selak, former leader of the Klamath Falls band and one of the best-known directors in Oregon, will lead the new organization.

There is a wealth of material available for forming a splendid organization, and plans are already under way to augment these with two or three first-class bandmen from outside points, for whom positions have been provided here.

During the same year, another local band was created in town by the local musician's union, called the Klamath Musician's Union Band (Evening Herald, 06-20-1931). It appears these two bands were operating simultaneously, and it is unclear how much overlap there might have been between them (Evening Herald, 07-11-1931; Evening Herald, 09-14-1931). The leader of the union band was S.V. Pickett (Evening Herald, 06-20-1931).

Despite the competition of two bands in town, the Klamath Falls Municipal Band was able to continue through the winter and into the next year. A new band leader, O.K. Cole, took charge in 1932 (Evening Herald, 05-05-1932; Evening Herald, 06-10-1932). The band played typical concerts around town and received support from some local businesses (Klamath News, 09-02-1932). The highlight of the season was a series of performances representing Klamath Falls at the Lakeview Roundup (Klamath News, 09-03-1932).

The Klamath Falls Municipal Band would have one more active season under the leadership of O.K. Cole in 1933 before becoming dormant for a few years. Supporters of the band attempted to again collect a subscription to support the band, and they even hoped that financing the band might become part of the city budget the following year. However, it would not be until 1936 that serious action was taken on the formation of the band (Evening Herald, 07-20-1933)

Evening Herald July 20, 1933
"The Municipal Band Seeks Aid"

There is in Klamath Falls a municipal band and its modesty has only been surpassed by its excellent concert talent. The organization of musicians has been quietly struggling along for several years, but this year it has received a helping hand from the public. The Junior Chamber of Commerce, an organization of alert young men, has volunteered its assistance, and will cooperate with a citizens committee in supporting the band. A campaign has been developed to raise funds to finance a series of public concerts, equip the organization, purchase music and instruments, and incidental expenses. This drive for subscriptions is the first and last the band will ask, the committee tells us. The amount required is small; the functions of a band numerous. These musicians have volunteered their services willingly for all occasions. The band maybe placed on the city budget next year, but until then it must depend upon the public subscription. The Chamber of Commerce office will receive any donations for this movement.

It is most likely that community "pick-up" bands were active from 1933-1936 for various local events, however, it would not be until 1936 that serious talk about an official organization would take place again. During this year, a city measure appeared that suggested a levy to provide financial support for a city band (Evening Herald, 04-23-1936).

The charter amendment for this proposal read as follows:

Evening Herald May 2, 1936
"Charter Amendment Submitted to the Voters by the Common Council"

An act to amend the Charter of the City of Klamath Falls, by adding thereto Chapter 8 authorizing the Common Council to levy and collect a tax of four-tenths of a mill upon each dollar of all taxable property in the City of Klamath Falls, Oregon, each year, beginning with the tax levy to be made in 1936, for the support, maintenance, pay and equipment, exclusive of instruments, of a band of music to be known as the Klamath Falls Municipal Band; creating a special fund of said City to be known as the Klamath Falls Municipal Band Fund, and providing that all funds derived from the tax levies herein provided for shall be covered into such fund; repealing all tax limitations contained in said Charter insofar as said levy is concerned; said band shall at all times consist of at least twenty pieces, and all funds levied or assessed therefor shall be under exclusive control of the Common Council.

Klamath's Municipal Band

This is a picture of the Klamath Falls municipal band, for which a supporting levy will be on the ballot this Friday. Left right, front to back: F. Penrod, W. Hornshuh, F. Silani, J. Solonberger, R. Bigger, Nathan. Second column: J. Nelson, V. Michaelson, C. Lansinger, D. Sellers, G. Fiske. Third column: C. Farrell, F. Glover, F. Solak, J. Telford. Fourth column: F. Berglund, R. Morgan, A. Reed, D. West, W. Sevits and Director Raymond Coopey. (Herald-News Photo-engraving).

The Klamath Falls Municipal Band
Evening Herald, May 11, 1936

Evening Herald May 11, 1936
"Band Included in Three City Ballot Issues"

On the ballot Friday will be three city measures, one of them providing for .4 of a mill levy for a municipal band. A group of local men and women is supporting the band levy, and providing information for the public prior to the decision on this measure Friday. They state that there is considerable misunderstanding of the measure of a .4 of a mill levy. This tax would mean a cost of 40 cents per thousand dollars of assessed valuation of all property and would make $3600 available yearly for maintenance of the band, assuming complete collection of taxes. While the band had an original sponsorship in the Elks lodge, it is definitely not an Elks band. The purpose is to provide a community band, which will be available for all sorts of public functions. Under the plan, a non-salaried committee of three, to be appointed by the city council, is to supervise the disbursement of the funds and appoint the officers of the band, as listed in the budget. Free concerts are planned once a month during winter and bi-monthly during the summer, the latter to be out of doors. Supporters of the band movement state that the musicians' union favors the program as it is laid out. They list benefits to be derived from a band as follows: filling of civic need, satisfaction of civic pride, practical saving, educational advantage, cultural stimulation to the community, entertainment value and equitable distribution of the support of the band. Salem, Albany, Grants Pass, Ashland, and La Grande are listed as Oregon cities with municipal bands. The saving angle is stressed in the statement being distributed in behalf of the band levy. It is recalled that some years ago a band was "imported" for a local event at a cost of $2600. Schools of Klamath Falls, it is pointed out, are spending considerable sums of money each year in instructions in band playing and have hundreds of dollars invested in instruments. Proficient bandsmen in the schools will graduate into the municipal band. Regular concerts and appearances of a band will inevitably stimulate more interest among adults and children in music, it is argued. Supporters of the band say that bands have been organized a good many times here, with the support of business houses of the city. "It is well to remember that those who derive the greatest share of enjoyment, educational and cultural value are not the business houses that have supported bands in the past, but the entire populace," the statement remarks, in support of the theory of financing the band by tax levy.

The tax levy passed with 1,812 "yes" votes and 1,218 "No" votes (Evening Herald, 05-22-1936). The funds for the band would not kick in until the following year, but the band remained active throughout 1936 under the direction of Raymond Coopey. It was promised at this point that the band would remain active through the winter, which is something that had never happened up until this point (Klamath News, 09-30-1936).

As promised, the band made appearances even during winter, performing for the opening of the "Weed-Klamath" road and for Armistice Day ceremonies in November (Klamath News, 10-06-1936; Evening Herald, 11-11-1936). The next year, however, controversy would begin to stir regarding band finances. In a letter to the editor of the Klamath News, R.C. Hoskinson decried the fact that the municipal band was going to charge $650 for its services in the Buckaroo Days celebration occurring that year. Hoskinson was understandably upset that a civic organization supported by a local tax would charge money to appear in a local event. This was especially egregious considering the fact that the American Legion drum corps and Eagles drum corps were donating their services for the event (Klamath News, 07-03-1937).

After a normal schedule of performances from 1937-1938, the money controversy would come to a climax when the Central Labor Council proposed combining levies for the band, parks, and recreation into one general purpose levy that could be used to fund multiple recreational activities, rather than be restricted to one or two specific organizations (Evening Herald, 04-14-1938).

The proposed resolution, seen below, stemmed directly from the charges that local organizations were having to pay for the band to appear in local community events.

Evening Herald July 14, 1938
"Two Mill Levy Plan Proposed"

"Whereas the city of Klamath Falls does maintain a 1/2 mill levy for the purpose of maintaining a municipal band and Whereas this band is created for the sole purpose of supplying music for the various functions held within the municipality of the city of Klamath Falls and Whereas, the Rodeo association of Klamath county is but a municipal affair, only going outside the city limits because of the fact that the city of Klamath Falls has no grounds suitable for the functions of the rodeo association and Whereas, we, the Klamath Falls Central Labor Union have been informed that the band, for which this said tax levy has been made has placed a charge on its services in the sum of $720.00 for furnishing music appropriate to the occasion and Whereas, we feel that inasmuch as this band is being supported by the general public through the tax levy paid by the property owners of this county and

Whereas, the American Legion drum corps and the auxiliary to the Fraternal Order of Eagles drum corps has cooperated 100 per cent in offering their services to make the affair of the community a success and whereas, the park board carries a levy of one mill for its needs and the recreation committee also receives a 1/2 mill levy together with the 1/2 mill levy for the maintenance of the municipal band thus making a total of two mills that are levied within our city for one purpose. Now therefore, be it resolved by this Klamath Falls Central Labor union that the laws be so amended to have a two mill levy made for one purpose only and that it be known as recreation levy. This levy to be budgeted into several funds as required and be it further resolved, that there shall be but one board to administer such funds as required and that this board be known as the recreation board and that the functions of the park board, the municipal band, and the present recreation committee be placed in the hands of this said new recreation board whose duties shall be to take care of the funds created by the two mills of levy now on the statutes and to portion out to the various activities that part necessary to cause the respective departments to function properly, and be it further resolved, that copies of this resolution be sent to the Hon. Mayor Clifton Richmond and to the city council, also that a copy be sent to the director of the municipal band, the park board and to the recreation committee and that a copy be submitted to the public press and to radio station KFJI for publication, with the idea in view of creating public interest in this matter."

Despite this suggestion, business went on as usual from 1938 through 1940 with weekly summer concerts and performances for Memorial Day and other holidays (Evening Herald, 08-24-1938; Evening Herald, 05-29-1939; Evening Herald, 08-27-1940). The situation would come up again in late 1940, with a letter from the band urging the community to reject the amendment that had been proposed some two years earlier (Klamath News, 11-03-1940).

Klamath News November 3, 1940
"Band Members Urge Refusal of City Bill"

Members of the municipal band made a statement Saturday urging defeat of the charter amendment repealing the band fund, to be on the ballot November 5. The statement follows: The charter amendment establishing the municipal band fund which was passed by the voters of Klamath Falls in 1936 by an overwhelming majority of four to one, is again upon the ballot for consideration at the coming election. According to records on file at the city hall, the band has made some 65 appearances during its existence, including concerts, parades, conventions, patriotic celebrations, and civic programs. A series of summer concerts has been presented each year to an estimated audience of 3000 people. As an educational organization, the band is giving additional training and experience to young musicians during and after their graduation from the local high school. More than 40 youths have availed themselves of this opportunity to play alongside more experienced musicians in the past few years. Much valuable training would be lost to them and to others in the future should the band be discontinued. The older-in-years members find in the band an opportunity to continue the playing for which they have been trained. Many of them do not wish to do solo or concert work, nor do they wish to participate in dance band activities, but they do wish to make use of the training and skill developed at the cost of time and money in earlier years. Thus men employed in other means of livelihood find an opportunity to be of service to their community. The proposition to be voted on Tuesday is a charter amendment which would divert the funds of the band to recreation purposes. Presumably the funds would then be used for the development of projects similar to the softball field which was undertaken by the recreation committee this last summer. Klamath voters who wish to have the band continued should vote against the proposed charter amendment. MEMBERS OF THE BAND.

It appears that the community voted in favor of the band and rejected the amendment to combine funds into an all-purpose recreation fund. The following year, considerable effort was made to show that the band was "active' and contributing "valuable service to the community" (Evening Herald, 01-20-1941). The band elected a new bandleader, Charles Stanfield, who also worked as band director for the high school. At the same time, big plans were being made for the coming season, including a bandstand in Moore Park and new uniforms for the band (Evening Herald, 01-20-1941). The year 1941 was indeed a very a busy year for the band with weekly concerts, multiple parade performances, fundraisers for the local swimming pool, and even an experimentation with performances between boxing/wrestling matches at the Klamath Armory (Evening Herald, 06-04-1941; Klamath News, 06-24-1941; Evening Herald; 06-24-1941).

Everything would change in 1942. Nothing could prepare the community for what was coming at the end of 1941: the attack on Pearl Harbor and the start of U.S. involvement in World War II. It seems local officials did not believe they could justify tax support for a band during this time, and they felt that resources should be contributed to public safety instead. In March of 1942, it was suggested that the band levy be replaced by a different levy to be used in "increasing manpower and equipment for the police department" (Klamath News, 03-25-1942). The proposal mentioned that, "what is intended is that the .4 of a mill band levy should be repealed, and the money used instead for the police department in this emergency period" (Klamath News, 03-25-1942).

The charter amendment for this action read as follows:

Klamath News May 7, 1942
"Charter Amendment Submitted to the Voters by the Common Council"

Shall the charter of the City of Klamath Falls be amended by repealing Chapter 8, authorizing levy of a four tenths of a mill tax upon taxable property for the support, maintenance, pay and equipment of the Klamath Falls Municipal Band, and in lieu thereof to amend the charter of the City of Klamath Falls by adding thereto Chapter 16, authorizing the Common Council to levy a tax of four tenths of a mill upon each dollar of taxable property in the City of Klamath Falls, Oregon, to be used for the increase in man power of the City Police Department, the purchase of new emergency equipment, improvement in the sanitation, ventilation and renovation of the City Jail; creating a special fund to be known as the "Emergency Police Fund;" repealing any and all provisions of said charter in conflict herewith and repealing all tax limitations contained in said charter as to this levy."

Though the events surrounding World War II are not specifically mentioned in the charter amendment, it is easy to see how those events would impact these financial decisions. The amendment was successful, though it seems it did not go through until 1944, and what were funds for the municipal band ultimately went to an "Emergency Police Fund." This decision pretty much put the nail in the coffin for the municipal band for a period of six years or so. It was not until 1950 that official efforts to organize a band would surface again (Herald and News, 04-11-1950).

Herald and News April 11, 1950
"Band Revivers Seek City Financial Aid, Request Levy Be Put on Ballot"

The old city band - once part and parcel of balmy summer evenings in Klamath Falls, has been reorganized, but that old bugaboo, money, is needed to put the band on a sound basis. For that reason - the money angle - two members of the revitalized band, Bob Chilcote and Director Freeman Yount, approached the city council with a scheme for raising sustaining funds. Chilcote, speaking for the group, asked council assistance in placing an eight-tenths mill levy on November general election ballots and securing interim financial aid from the city till July, 1951. The group also asked appointment of a band commission by the mayor and council to supervise the organization. General council opinion seemed to favor the plan, and Chilcote was asked to address his requests to the council budget committee by letter. Yearly cost: Chilcote estimated the yearly cost of maintaining a 40-piece concert band in the neighborhood of $7980. Included in his estimate was compensation of band members for 33 concerts and 52 rehearsals and $3 each for each concert. Along with that was added $300 each for conductor and business manager salaries and the purchase of music. Chilcote stated the only way to assure a good band was to pay its members. He said during an eight-year period from May 15, 1936 to May 10, 1944, the former city band was supported by a four-tenths mill levy. When the band was disbanded in 1944 the fund was abolished and put into a city jail sinking fund. Chilcote estimated that under present city land evaluation the four-tenths of a mill levy would raise $5600. Councilman Alfred Condrey suggested that the disposition of the former city band fund, which was converted to the city jail sinking fund be investigated with a view to interim financing of the reorganized group.

For the year of 1950, the municipal band was back with a bang under the direction of Freeman Yount. Weekly concerts returned once again to much fanfare and public support (Herald and News, 04-14-1950; Herald and News, 07-08-1950; Herald and News, 07-15-1950, Herald and News, 07-22-1950; Herald and News, 08-12-1950).

As promised, the band put forward a proposal to once again pass a tax levy for support of the band.

The proposal was as follows:

Herald and News October 16, 1950 "Resolution No. 427"

A resolution providing for a levy of six tenths of a mill upon the dollar of all taxable property in the City of Klamath Falls, Oregon, beginning with the 1951-1952 budget and tax year and each year thereafter, to be used to support a municipal band, including expense of organizing, equipping and maintaining same and the paying salaries of instructors and members thereof: amending the city charter of the City of Klamath Falls, so said objectives and purposes may be accomplished: calling a special election for the purpose of voting upon the matter providing a ballot title for the question to be submitted and directing the posting and publication of election notices.

Advertisement for the Klamath Falls Municipal Band
Herald and News, November 4, 1950

Unfortunately, the new band levy failed to win public support. The measure failed with 1,572 "Yes" Votes and 3,191 "No" Votes. An editorial in the Herald and News reported that this indicated that "Klamath Falls residents don't intend to tax themselves to support anyone's hobby" (Herald and News, 11-09-1950).

This little jab at the band was not taken lightly, and Freeman Yount, director of the band, replied with a letter to the editor:

Herald and News November 16, 1950
"Freeman Yount Letter to the Editor"

Gentleman: When the Klamath Falls municipal band gave its first winter season concert on Oct. 31st, you failed to print the program or give it adequate public notice. In last Thursday's paper you editorialized your report of the defeat of the measure to support a permanent municipal band by saying "the voters were not about to tax themselves for the support of anyone's hobby." How have we deserved this unnecessarily vindictive treatment? Let's get it straight. None of us ever dreamed of asking the people to tax themselves for the support of his hobby. You could not better have misrepresented the case. We believed that we had something of value to sell to the people of this city, and the price tag on it was not high. We offered a year around series of free concerts and the enhancement of band music to our civic functions, at the same time providing an organization in which the high school graduate musicians could continue the musical skill acquired through so many years of hard work and at such cost in school taxes. Music in the schools has long since proved its great value, both in education and as one of the strongest factors in retention of juvenile and adult delinquency. But does it make any sense to train the student to a high degree of musical skill only to put his instrument away upon graduation because there is no band or orchestra in which he can play? The cities of Ashland, Bend, Roseburg and many other cities in Oregon and all other states maintain tax supported municipal bands. So did Klamath Falls until 1944. I think that the significant fact is that 1575 voters of our city were willing to tax themselves for this purpose. We shall do our best not to let them down. I do not know whether the musicians will give their time and work as a public service any more that you would hand out free newspapers for this purpose. Remember, to us it means giving up five nights each month and four afternoons in the summer. But I can assure you that for as long as the musicians turn out they will not be without a director.
Cordially yours, Freeman A. Yount.

Though it is probable that an ad-hoc organization of some kind of band for holidays and other special events would continue, this was effectively the end of the Klamath Falls Municipal Band. Some citizens took notice, decrying the silence of some festivities and events around town (Herald and News, 07-06-1960). However, 1950 would mark the end of an official city band in Klamath Falls.

Herald and News July 6, 1960 "Flabbergasted"

I was completely flabbergasted while watching the parade down Main Street. It was very colorful and well organized, but it was quiet. Too quiet. Very much like a funeral procession. The main thing with the lack of any type of brass band. In fact, it is the first Fourth of July parade I've seen in 43 years of watching them that there was little or no music. Is this city so poverty stricken, both monetarily and cultural speaking, that it can't even support a municipal band? I can imagine the impression all this made on out of town visitors. There were also many remarks apropos of this matter from many "men on the street." I would wager my last shilling that there are enough musicians in this town to organize a top-notch band, and to play just for the fun of it, without pay, or very nominal remuneration. Don't some of you readers of this letter have nostalgic memories of a band concert in the park on a warm Sunday afternoon? There is a trite phrase floating around to the effect "Oh, we have a high school band." But what chance does the middle-aged working man musician have to sit and play with the high school band? And when is the high school's band available during the summer months? Klamath Falls, this is a chance to work up some of that civic pride I hear so much about. If anybody is interested in an organization of this type, and perhaps a concert orchestra later, I would appreciate a card and if there is enough response, we can call a meeting, and maybe cook up something. Norman T. Hanson (Frustrated Flute Player).

LaMar Jensen's Starlighters and members from Baldy Evans' Band and Jack Pearson's Dance Masters, all three of which were prominent local dance bands, united in 1963 to pay homage to the American band tradition in Klamath Falls with an "Old-Time Sunday Band Concert" (Herald and News, 07-25-1963).

Herald and News July 25, 1963
"Old-Time Sunday Band Concert to be Revived"

It seems like only yesterday every town in the country had a band shell in the municipal park and Saturday was concert night. During the decades of the 20s and 30s, money was no status symbol. Nobody had any. The "big men" in town were the members of the band - farmers, merchants, neighbors - who donated their talents to provide free weekly entertainment. The grocer who rewarded payment of his bill with a sack of candy for the kids played trombone. The man who drove the ice wagon, with its long tail of barefoot children, was the drummer. When the old-time concert is revived Sunday, July 28, in Veteran's Memorial Park, Klamath Falls neighbors will be the music men. LaMar Jensen's Starlighters, enlarged into the greater Starlighters Concert Dance Band by musicians from Baldy's Band, and Jack Pearson's Dance Masters, will play the danceable tunes from the "only yesterday" era. Saxophonists are LaMar Jensen, school teacher; Roger Beck, millwright; Norman Beck, estimator; "Bud" Blanchard, car salesman, and Lawny Hallack, student. Trumpet section is composed of Fred Floetke, appliance store manager; David Johnson, bank loan officer; James Metler, accountant; Ephraim Hackett, teacher. Trombonists are Dr. R. F. Peters, optometrist, Dr. James L. Lawson, optometrist, and Dwight Schuck, student. Rhythm section is made up of Normand Poulshock, teacher; Ronald Jones, upholsterer; William J. Cunningham, car salesman; Ted M. Van, automotive parts man, and Richard Douglas, men's apparel salesman. Funds from the Recording and Transcription Industries make the concert possible, but the men who form the band are rehearsing long hours after their regular workday to assure its success.

Linkville in Ye Olde Times
Evening Herald 08-02-1923

Part 2: Social/Fraternal Organization Bands

Klamath Falls has been home to numerous bands that were organized by local members of national fraternities and social organizations. These groups were incredibly successful in their musical undertakings, even claiming championship titles in some cases. They were also very active in the local community, performing for a wide variety of parades and local celebrations. These groups represented the Klamath community just as much as the civic bands that were organized in the city. At times, some of these groups were actually thought of and treated as city bands.

This section explores the history of four major social organizations that organized musical groups at one time or another. These organizations include the Shrine Club (Hillah Temple Drum and Bugle Corps), the Elks (Elks Band/Elks Drum and Bugle Corps), the Eagles (Eagles Drum and Bugle Corps/Ladies Drum and Bugle Corps), and the American Legion Post No. 8 (Drum and Bugle Corps).

All of these groups brought attention to the Klamath community. The more obvious benefit of the groups was when they hosted state conventions for their respective organizations, bringing a host of tourists to the region. However, they also represented Klamath outside of the community as they attended state/national conventions and competitions. At times, local businesses and the chamber of commerce even supported these trips financially and equipped the bands with advertising material to hand out on their journeys.

Linkville in Ye Olde Times
Evening Herald **06-27-1923**

Shrine Club

The Shrine Club in Klamath Falls was established in 1925, and it quickly became an active organization in the community (Klamath News, 05-10-1928). Not long after the group started, they initiated their drum and bugle corps, which was called the Crater Lake Drum and Bugle Corps, or the Hillah Temple Drum and Bugle Corps (Evening Herald, 05-20-1925; Evening Herald, 05-23-1925). At times, they were referred to as a fife and drum corps as well (Evening Herald, 05-27-1925).

From the outset, this drum and bugle corps was seen as a community asset. One of the first activities of the group was a trip to the national Shriner convention in 1925. The community saw this trip as an opportunity to advertise the city of Klamath Falls (Evening Herald, 05-27-1925).

The appearance of this local group at the national convention was a big deal for the local community. Klamath community members were even able to participate by tuning into a broadcast of their performance on the radio. Even though the program was scheduled at midnight, many locals made special plans to tune in and celebrate the local group and their work to advertise the local community to a national audience (Evening Herald, 06-03-1925).

The drum and bugle corps continued to be active for several decades. They continued to represent Klamath Falls at conventions and other types of events, however, they also participated in numerous local events, fundraisers, and other activities (Klamath News, 04-10-1937; Klamath News, 07-28-1935; Evening Herald, 04-14-1937).

Evening Herald May 27, 1925
"Drum Corps to Advertise City on Trip South"

Armed with 10,000 board planks, members of the fife and drum corps of Klamath Falls, Hillah Temple, will leave on the Saturday morning train for Los Angeles to distribute free information and publicity about Klamath Falls and Klamath county at the national convention of the Mystic Shrine. The planks were the courtesy of the Shaw-Bertram Lumber company and the printing through the courtesy of the Klamath county chamber of commerce. It is the aim of the Klamath visitors in the south, according to W.C. Van Emon, president of the Crater Lake Shrine Club, to distribute the planks while en route south and in Los Angeles as well. On one side of the planks are the words Klamath: Lakes, Land, Livestock and Lumber: An empire Awakening." On the reverse side are the words: Hillah Temple Drum Corps, courtesy of Shaw-Bertram Lumber company and Klamath county chamber of commerce.

The Klamath men will leave Saturday morning to join the special Hillah train at Weed, which is made up in Medford. About 75 or 80 men are expected to make the trip to Los Angeles. Those making up the drum corps are J.O. Rhodes, captain; R.E. Crego, Ray Dunn, A.L. Wishard, I.J. Struble, Dr. Coe; bugle corps is composed of Hans Nylander, E.J. McLaughlin, N.G. Wheeler and A.E. Peasley. W.C. Van Emon will also make the trip.

Shrine Corps at the Balsiger Building
Herald and News, 11-14-1952

"Money for Hospital"
Evening Herald, 04-14-1937

Virgil Williams, major of the Hillah Temple drum corps which will parade in Klamath Falls Saturday afternoon in connection with the Shrine ceremonial here this weekend. The parade will start from the armory at 4:30 o'clock, swing down Main street and then march back to the armory. (Herald-News Photo-Engraving).

Shrine Corps Leader Virgil Williams
Evening Herald, 06-19-1936

**Shrine Corps Bass Drum
Klamath County Museum 2798.2013.020.0001**

LOS ANGELES, Cal.—John Philip Sousa, composer and band master, tried his hand at directing Broadway traffic here. Five minutes after he replaced the crossing cop the corner was a choked malestrom of tangled fenders heaving tempestuously to the hysterical bleating of automobile horns and the rhapsody in traffic simply would not keep time with movements of his baton.

Finally the director of brass bands called for help and walked out on his unruly tin orchestra. In less than an hour six traffic cops had straightened out the turbulent tangle and the flivvers once more moved placidly in their courses.

Sousa Directs Traffic
Evening Herald 01-17-1924

Elks

The Benevolent and Protective Order of Elks (B.P.O.E) was brought to Klamath Falls in 1911 (Klamath News, 05-10-1928; Evening Herald, 05-29-1911). The Klamath Falls Military Band played at a convention for the group around this time. Over time, the Elks would have a close relationship with the city bands by providing some support and rehearsal space. In 1914, however, the Elks formed their own band made up exclusively of members from the local lodge (Evening Herald, 03-20-1914).

Evening Herald March 20, 1914
"Elks Band is Given a Start"

Musicians are named on committee to whoop 'er up, and lodge expects to have 20 instrumentalists, all Elks. The All-Elks band suggestion has been received with great enthusiasm by members of the local lodge, and plans are now under way for the organization of a twenty-piece band. A committee was appointed at Thursday evening's session of the Elks Lodge to have charge of the matter, consisting of J.E. Bodge, Allen Sloan, C.M. Ramsby, Charles Martin, E.B. Henry, A.Y. Trudall, R.E. Mitchell, A.L. Wishard, Marion Barnes, Fred Houston, O.M. Hector, Chas. Mashburn, and George Tugnot.

At various points, the Elks band was actually considered a city band itself, even going by the name "Elks Municipal Band" at times (Evening Herald, 03-27-1936). The band remained active at least into the 1960s, and probably even longer. They performed for a wide variety of local parades, celebrations, and charitable events. The band was especially active in patriotic and military celebrations (Herald and News, 12-05-1963).

Elks Band at the Armory
Herald and News, **12-21-1959**

Elks Band
Herald and News, **12-09-1962**

ELKS BAND—Dick Gallagher steps out as leader of the Elks band which paced the 50th Anniversary parade down Main Street Saturday afternoon. A band concert Saturday, and a special dance Saturday night at the Elks Lodge wrapped up the Golden Anniversary celebration.

Elks Band on Parade in front of the Balsiger Building
Herald and News, 07-24-1961

In the summer of 1929, the local Elks also organized a drum and bugle corps for the initial purpose of performing at that year's Elks convention (Klamath News, 06-11-1929). This group only appears to have remained active for a couple years (Evening Herald, 10-23-1930).

Elks Band
Herald and News, 12-26-1963

Baby Elks
Klamath County Museum 2486.2013.020.0001

Elks Band in 1959
Klamath County Museum 2018.002.0170

Elks Band
Klamath County Museum 2018.002.0171

Elks Band
Klamath County Museum 2018.002.0172

Elks Band Parade
Klamath County Museum 2018.002.0169

Bad news from London. This city now maintains 90 municipal bands, in all of which are saxophones.

Tom Sims Says Bad News from London
Evening Herald 09-16-1924

Eagles

The Fraternal Order of Eagles was organized in Klamath Falls around 1926, and included a ladies' auxiliary group that formed in 1928 (Klamath News, 05-10-1928; Evening Herald, 06-29-1938). The Eagles' drum and bugle corps appears in local newspapers starting around 1930 (Klamath News, 01-23-1930).

The group was lauded for its abilities, even winning the state level championships multiple times and performing well in other contests (Klamath News, 07-07-1937; Evening Herald, 07-11-1939; Evening Herald, 07-08-1939). They also supplied music for a variety of local activities, such as dances, and worked closely, at times, with the Klamath Falls municipal band and other local entities (Evening Herald, 07-11-1939; Herald and News, 05-01-1937).

The success of the band captured the attention of the local community, and many local businesses contributed to the drum and bugle corps in an effort to bring the statewide convention to Klamath Falls in 1938. There is little doubt that these businesses also felt that this award-winning drum and bugle corps was an excellent advertisement for the local community.

Eagles Drum Corps on Parade
Klamath News, 06-13-1937

Eagles Drum Corps
Evening Herald, 07-09-1940

A "Drum-Majorette" contest was included in this effort, with seven local women competing for the honor of serving as a drum major for the group at the statewide competition (Evening Herald, 06-11-1937). The contest was won by Lucille McAninch who was sponsored by the Klamath Falls police department (Evening Herald, 06-14-1937). A similar competition was held to help sponsor a trip to a championship event in San Francisco in 1939 (Evening Herald, 07-08-1939).

Applicant Photos for the Lady Drum Major Contest
Evening Herald, 06-11-1937

Advertisement for the Lady Drum Major Contest
Evening Herald, 05-20-1937

The Ladies' Auxiliary Eagles group also had a drum corps of their own (Herald and News, 12-03-1945). This auxiliary group boasted Oregon's only all-female drum corps at the time (Evening Herald, 06-29-1938). They were active in local events and celebrations and went on to become state-champions in 1940 (Evening Herald 07-05-1940).

The Lady Eagles Drum Corps
Klamath County Museum 2019.002.0224

Both the Eagles Drum Corps and the Lady Eagles Auxiliary Drum Corps were active into the early 1950s. Though a brief reorganization for the auxiliary group appears in the early 1960s, the groups would effectively come to an end in the early 1950s (Herald and News, 04-28-1953; Herald and News, 10-24-1961).

The Lady Eagles Drum Corps
Evening Herald, 07-05-1940

The Lady Eagles Drum Corps
Evening Herald, **06-29-1938**

Members of Lady Eagles Auxiliary Drum Corps
Herald and News, **10-22-1947**

Mrs. Cecile Otto on Parade with the Lady Eagles Drum Corps
Herald and News, 11-24-1951

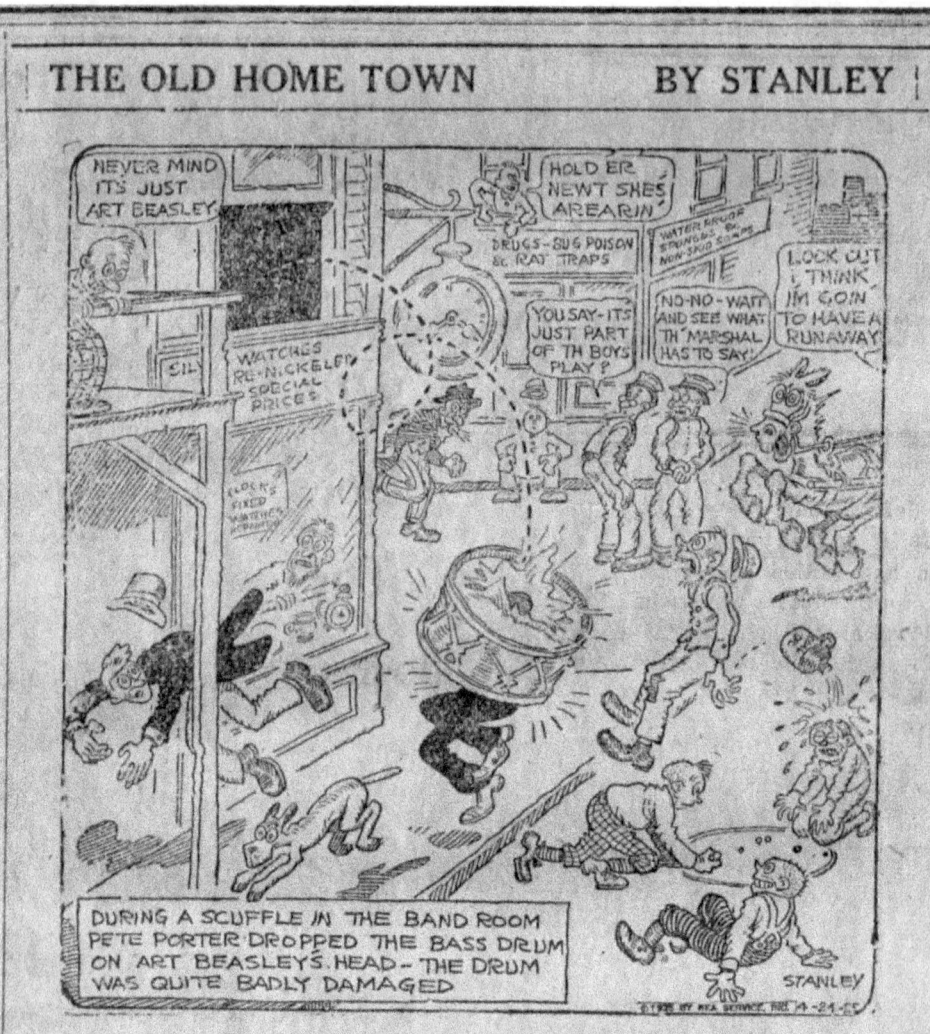

The Old Hometown Cartoon
Evening Herald, 05-06-1925

American Legion

The American Legion Drum and Bugle Corps was organized in Klamath Falls in 1923 under the leadership of Roy Everhart (Evening Herald, 02-12-1923). The group attended a convention in San Francisco and earned fourth place for their performance (Evening Herald, 10-19-1923).

Evening Herald October 19, 1923
"Some Post, Klamath No. 8"

Some Achievement for the American Legion drum and bugle corps to take fourth place at San Francisco! It should, and does, make every Klamath citizen proud of them. Competing with cities ten times, and more, the size of this; cities that backed their men to the limit with funds and encouragement, the local post's musical organization stepped right out toward the head of the column. It was a remarkable showing of indomitable spirit. Sheer resolve to put it over is responsible for the accomplishment, and the whole credit is due to the men within the post. The spirit that put them in the top rank is the spirit displayed by the leader and director, Roy Everhart, who should have been in the hospital, but jeopardized health and even life to be with the organization. Sheer will-power sustained him, nothing else. It was a fine thing for the community that the boys put over, and a fine thing for the post. It shows an esprit de corps in the post that accomplishes things that to the ordinary mind might seem impossible. It's a good sort of spirit to have in a community, and sets a good example for the rest of us to follow.

The Legion drum and bugle corps quickly set their sights even higher as they planned to attend the national convention in St. Paul, Minnesota the very next year (Evening Herald, 01-17-1924). It is unclear whether the group was able to raise the funds needed for the trip, and for the next few years, the drum and bugle corps mainly participated in local parades and other events. For a time in the late 1920s and early 1930s, the Legion drum corps combined with the Elks drum corps for some events (Klamath News, 09-04-1929). However, the group was relatively inactive for several years.

Despite the early success of the group, it appears that a reorganization was required in 1933 with new equipment and membership. This was mainly instigated by the fact that the state level convention for the American Legion was taking place in Klamath Falls that year (Klamath News, 01-19-1933). Later that year, Dewey Powell served as drum major and Roland T. Warren took over as president for the group (Klamath News, 03-02-1933).

The American Legion Drum Corps on Main Street
Klamath County Museum 2486.2008.070.0008

Drum Major Dewey Powell
Evening Herald, 07-01-1936

In an effort to raise funds for the new group, the drum and bugle corps hosted a series of dances and special concerts with some popular dance bands (Evening Herald, 10-17-1933). With the influx of these funds, the group was able to obtain new uniforms and become more active in the city (Evening Herald, 05-29-1934).

Advertisement for New Uniforms
Evening Herald, 05-29-1934

With the American Legion Drum and Bugle Corps, Klamath Falls had yet another musical group that they could use to advertise and "show-off" to other communities. The chamber of commerce would even sponsor some trips for the group to other cities (Klamath News, 06-01-1934). The group would not disappoint the local community as they took first place at the 1934 state level convention in Astoria (Evening Herald, 08-25-1934). With their success, a trip to another national convention was soon talk of the town (Evening Herald, 08-27-1934).

The following year, the corps would lose the state level competition at The Dalles by .15 of a point.

The group would bounce back the very next year, however, once again taking the state champion title at the 1936 state convention in Roseburg (Evening Herald, 08-29-1936). With this achievement, the chamber of commerce would help send the group to San Francisco to participate in the Golden Gate Fiesta Parade, where they earned first prize for their performance in the event (Evening Herald, 05-13-1937; Klamath News, 11-12-1937).

Legion Drum Corps After Convention
Klamath News, 08-18-1935

Drum Corps Extra! *Klamath Legionnaire Publication*, 07-12-1935
Klamath County Museum 1708.2012.053.0002

Drum Majoress Signe Pearson and Drum Major Dewey Powell, on a San Francisco street on the occasion of the Legion drum corps' successful appearance in the Golden Gate Bridge parade.

Dewey Powell and Signe Pearson in San Francisco Parade
Evening Herald, 01-01-1938

American Legion State Champions
Evening Herald, 08-29-1936

"Here Are Your Tickets, Sir"
Evening Herald, 05-13-1937

The Legion drum and bugle corps would again take the state championship in 1937, even bringing along a "junior drum and bugle corps" with them to the convention in Albany (Klamath News, 09-04-1937). With three state titles in their four years of competition, talk was now very serious about an attempt at a national title at the 1938 national convention in Los Angeles (Klamath News, 11-12-1937).

On To Los Angeles

DANCE

Let's Put Klamath Falls Over
in Los Angeles With the

**AMERICAN LEGION
DRUM CORPS**

ARMORY

Saturday, May 21

Music
BALDY EVANS AND HIS BAND
$1.00 Per Couple

Advertisement for Baldy's Dance Fundraiser for Legion
Evening Herald, 05-18-1938

A series of dances and other events were held to help raise funds to send the group to Los Angeles (Evening Herald, 05-18-1938). After yet another win at the 1938 state convention in Pendleton, a trip to Los Angeles was certain. The chamber of commerce prepared pine board souvenirs that were stamped with a "wooden box man," pelican, and a Klamath potato for the group to take with them (Klamath News, 09-03-1938; Evening Herald, 09-16-1938).

American Legion Drum and Bugle Corps at the L.A. Coliseum
Klamath County Museum 0041.2012.002.0108

After their trip to California, the American Legion drum corps would perform for the funeral ceremonies for O.C. Applegate (Evening Herald, 10-14-1938), who had been an Indian Agent, Pioneer and Modoc War Veteran.

The American Legion drum and bugle corps would go on to win another state championship at Salem in 1939. In addition to the group's achievements, several individual members received honors for their contributions to the drum and bugle corps. Drum Major Dewey Powell won the state championship for his role as drum major, while bugler S.V. Pickett and drummer Joe Solienberger also won state championships for their respective roles (Evening Herald, 08-16-1939).

In lieu of the state championships, the drum and bugle corps changed it up in 1940 by entering a competition in Northern California at the Shasta dam (Evening Herald, 05-08-1940). This event included a drum-majorette competition, which was undertaken by Neva McAnnulty (Klamath News, 05-29-1940). The corps won first place, while Neva tied for third place

Pageantry Marks Applegate Funeral

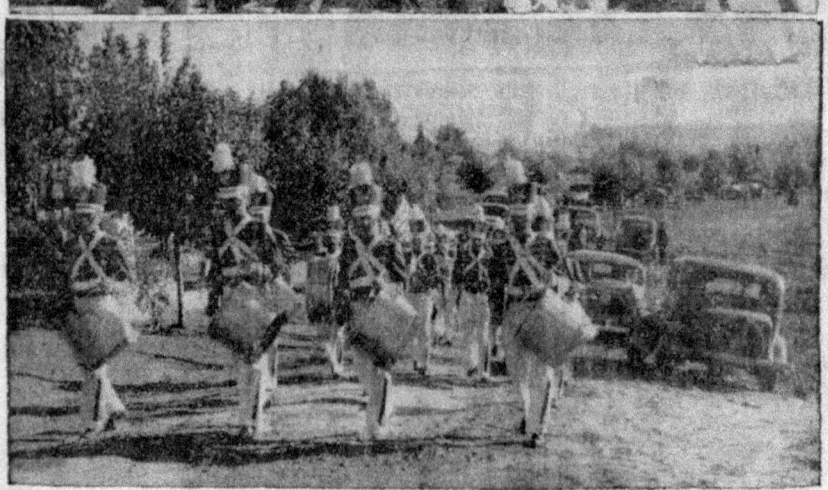

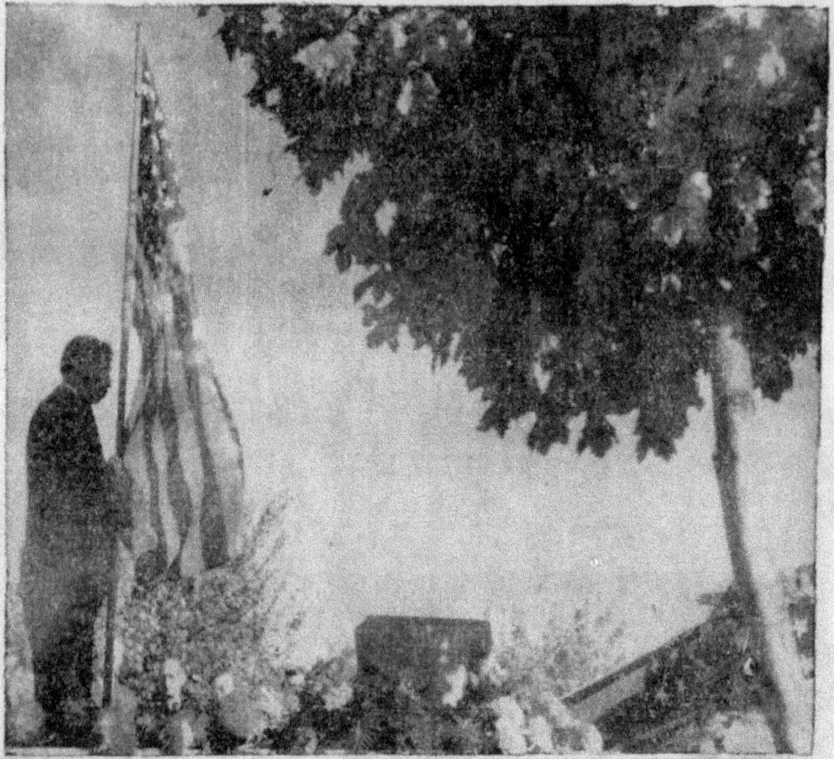

Above, Jim Johnson, Klamath Indian, holding a large American flag at the graveside services for Captain Oliver C. Applegate Thursday. Below, the American Legion drum corps, playing a funeral dirge, leads the procession up the hill to the cemetery. The Masonic lodge had charge of graveside services.

O.C. Applegate Funeral Photos

***Evening Herald*, 10-14-1938**

(Evening Herald, 06-03-1940). Though they were also invited to make an appearance at fairs in Sacramento and San Francisco, lack of finances prevented these opportunities from happening (Evening Herald, 08-24-1940).

The group received second place in this competition in 1941 (Evening Herald, 06-05-1941). They also made a return to the state convention held in Eugene that year (Klamath News, 07-13-1941).

After some activity for local events through 1943, the Legion drum and bugle corps disbanded at the outset of World War II. Members were encouraged to join again when the group tried to reorganize in 1946, but their first real performance did not occur until 1947 and this organization did not last past this point (Herald and News, 01-28-1946; Herald and News, 10-07-1947). Another effort to reorganize occurred in 1952, once again in response to the fact that the state convention was coming to Klamath Falls that year (Herald and News, 03-17-1952).

The group went on to win the state championship yet again in 1953 (Herald and News, 06-26-1953). They would also go on to defend their title in 1954, 1955, and 1956, repeating the success they had in the 1930s (Herald and News, 07-17-1954; Herald and News, 08-07-1955; Herald and News, 08-17-1956).

RAT-A-TAT-TAT went the American Legion Drum Corps down Main Street Tuesday, marching in the Armistice Day parade to the courthouse where the ceremony was held that marked the end of World War I.

Armistice Day Parade
Herald and News, 11-12-1952

Herald and News June 26, 1953
"Falls Drum and Buglers Amaze Selves by Capturing Trophy"

Klamath Legionnaires last week took the first long step toward getting back in an old familiar rut- The winning of the Legion's state championship for drum and bugle corps. Back in 1939, after the Klamath Corps had walked off with the championship five out of six years, winning permanent possession of the championship cup, the Klamathites turned the cup over to Salem's Post 9 to be entered in competition again. And the Klamath Corps disbanded, apparently to give other state posts a chance at the cup. Early last spring, as Legionnaires here began planning for the state convention held here last summer, they decided to form another corps to take part in the convention. It was such a long shot that no one even mentioned the possibility of recapturing the state championship with the new corps. Hillsboro's fine corps was the defending champion and appeared headed for more championships.

Hillsboro did win here again last year and immediately began preparing for a big third win this year which would give them permanent possession of the cup. But the Klamath Falls outfit declared Hillsboro should at least be challenged and almost nightly rehearsals began here. At the Seaside state convention last week almost anyone except the Klamath corpsmen would have bet you the family jewels against a handful of stale popcorn that Hillsboro would waltz to the third championship. But the Klamath Legionnaires blithely ignored the form chart and snappily took the championship away from Hillsboro. The new corps was organized here under leadership of Jack Benner, Warner Fett, Mike Eittreim, and Post Commander Dick Gallagher.

THE KLAMATH FALLS LEGION drum and bugle corps is shown marching down Main Street in one of the many parades in which it has participated. Drum Major Dick Gallagher is hidden behind the color guard which is leading the unit. The corps will defend its state title at Redmond during the annual Oregon Legion convention July 27-30.

Parade Photo
Herald and News, 07-24-1955

FUN HATS AND TROPHIES won at the recent state convention by Klamath Falls Post, No. 8, American Legion Drum Corps, which topped state competition at Seaside, draped the stage, (above) during a dinner at the Willard Hotel honoring the winners. To the left of stage, is Bud Steinseifer, president of the post; bending, George Baumgardner; seated left, Anna Steinseifer and Betty Ezell; right side of table, Post Commander Richard Gallagher and Stanley Ezell; Seated on stage, Frank Otto. Lower picture, (l to r) Bob Dannelley, Betty Tirres, Maxine Baumgardner and George Baumgardner.

Trophy Photos
Herald and News, 07-18-1953

Corps Photo
Herald and News, 08-07-1955

Photo at the Weed Italian Festival
Herald and News, 09-16-1956

The drum and bugle corps decreased in activity for several years before they were able to win second place at the state convention in Medford, where they went by the name "The Headliners" (Herald and News, 06-29-1961). Their activities continued to decline in the years that followed, essentially marking the end of the organization.

SATURDAY'S PARADE, sponsored by the Klamath Junior Chamber of Commerce in cooperation with the Klamath Merchants Association, will feature a number of musical units, including the American Legion Drum and Bugle Corps shown above behind the organization's color guard in the July 4 parade. Among other musical units participating are bands from Klamath Union, Henley and Butte Valley high schools and from OTI, plus the Leona Robertson accordion band. Today is the last day to mail entries for the December 6 event to Klamath Jaycees Parade Chairman, P.O. Box 407, Klamath Falls.

Fourth of July Parade Photo
Herald and News, **12-03-1958**

Evening Herald, January 24, 1941
"Twirl for the Twirlers"
There's a lot of conversation,
And a lot of cogitation,
And a bit of speculation
'Bout those strutting majorettes.
There's no end of agitation
Some amount of perturbation
And a lot of admiration
For those wriggling majorettes.
People say their dress is scanty,
But I think they are just "ranty,"
Cause they really look enchanty
As they step with booted feet.
Always full in time and smiling,
Flashing teeth and face beguiling,
And a study in smart styling
Strutting bravely down the street.
Young and strong and clean and snappy,
Healthy virulent, and happy.
Always full of pep and scrappy,
Gracious to whom e'er they meet.
Full possessed of charm and beauty,
Realizing well their duty,

Never snobbish, never snooty,
Diplomatic and discreet.
Knowing how thru hours of drilling
What to do, and always willing,
Good and well their job fulfilling,
Bowing never to defeat.
I have marched 'Neath sun, bright gleaming
With the perspiration streaming,
And with lots of hope and dreaming
Of a good place to sit down.
And I've lost all thoughts "paradey,"
As a plucky little lady
Who prayed for a spot all shady
Led our outfit down through town.
So, I say to all who chide them,
Let them try to march beside them,
Then perhaps they would abide them,
And could learn a lot of things.
And I wouldn't fear for betting,
That they'd feel naught but regretting,
And they'd say all majoretting
Were like angels without wings.
-L.C. Carr, Legion Drum Corps

Part 3: Bands from Outlying Communities

Klamath Falls was not alone in its desire to advertise its community through music. Many of the outlying communities in the region had their very own bands at different points in time. This feature was a staple of the typical American community, and the Klamath Basin had plenty of examples of this American spirit.

For many of these communities, the local school band often served as the town band, but some also had adult bands at one point or another. These groups constantly traveled to neighboring towns and performed with other groups. Included in this section are some highlights for different community groups within a fifty mile or so radius from Klamath Falls.

Linkville in Ye Olde Times Cartoon
Evening Herald, 05-14-1923

Merrill Brass Band

Merrill Band
Klamath County Museum 2017.002.7586

The Merrill Brass Band first appears in local news sources in the early 1900s with an advertisement for a grand Fourth of July celebration and dance to be held at the Merrill Opera House (Klamath Republican, 06-08-1905). They also appeared in partnership with neighboring groups for some events (Klamath Republican, 06-07-1906). Though they do not appear in the local newspaper frequently, mention of a Merrill Band does continue into the 1920s and beyond (Evening Herald, 12-20-1922).

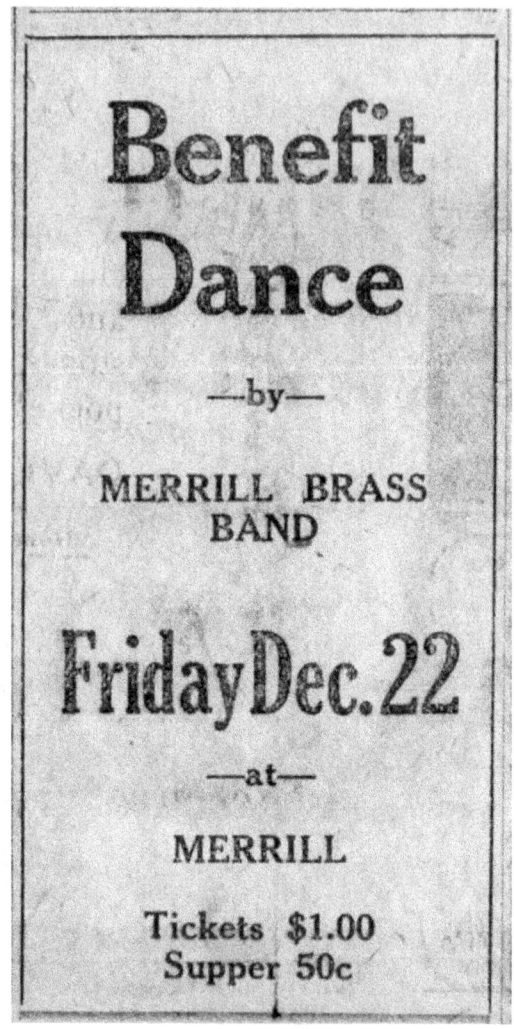

Advertisement for Dance
Evening Herald, **12-20-1922**

The group mainly hosted dances for their local community, but they also participated in regional events (Evening Herald, 01-02-1923; Evening Herald, 04-25-1940). When a local band was not organized, the Merrill High School band served as the town band (Herald and News, 12-16-1963; Herald and News, 12-22-1963).

Malin Brass Band

Malin also had a band, called the Sokol Brass Band of Malin, which emerged in the 1920s (Evening Herald, 03-04-1925). The group hosted dances in the local community.

Advertisement for Dance
Evening Herald, 03-04-1925

Fort Klamath

Fort Klamath developed a town band to compete with the Klamath Falls Municipal Band in 1931 (Evening Herald, 03-19-1931; Klamath News, 09-25-1931). Interestingly, at this time, Fred Seelak served as bandleader for both the Forth Klamath and Klamath Falls bands (Evening Herald, 03-19-1931).

Evening Herald March 19, 1931
"Fort Klamath Now Has 21-Piece Band"

Fort Klamath has recently formed a 21-piece band which will be under the direction of Prof. F.A. Selak, who is also instructor of the Klamath Falls municipal band. Holton instruments were furnished for the Fort Klamath band by the Shepherd Music company of this city. The Fort Klamath bandsmen have challenged the Klamath Falls band to a contest this summer to determine which is the better band.

Dorris

At times, the Klamath Falls band provided music for some events in Dorris, such as the arrival of the railroad (Evening Herald, 04-17-1908). However, these photos from the Klamath County Museum archives suggest that Dorris had its own band at one point.

Dorris Band
Klamath County Museum 2017.002.3516a

Dorris Band
Klamath County Museum 2017.002.3516b

Bonanza Band

Bonanza contributed a brass band to help celebrate Railroad Day in Klamath Falls in 1909 (Evening Herald, 05-20-1909). Later on, the town organized a band in 1913 that was meant to participate in a number of town events and celebrations. (Evening Herald, 12-15-1913).

Bonanza Community Club
Klamath County Museum 0016.1966.066.1936

Klamath Agency

In the early 1900s, a band was organized at the Klamath Agency. It was called the Klamath Agency Band, or sometimes the Klamath Agency Indian Band (Klamath Republican, 08-27-1903). This group performed with other school groups as well as the Klamath Falls band for baseball games and Fourth of July celebrations (Klamath Republican, 08-27-1903; Klamath Republican, 04-02-1908).

Superintendent's house at Klamath Agency
Klamath County Museum 0016.1966.066.0735

Keno

The Keno Band was active in the early 1900s. They hosted dances and even offered steamboat excursions on Upper Klamath Lake, in an effort to imitate the success that the Klamath Falls Military Band had with these types of events (Klamath Republican, 09-12-1907; Klamath Republican, 04-30-1908).

Keno Gospel Center
Klamath County Museum 0016.1955.16b.478.47

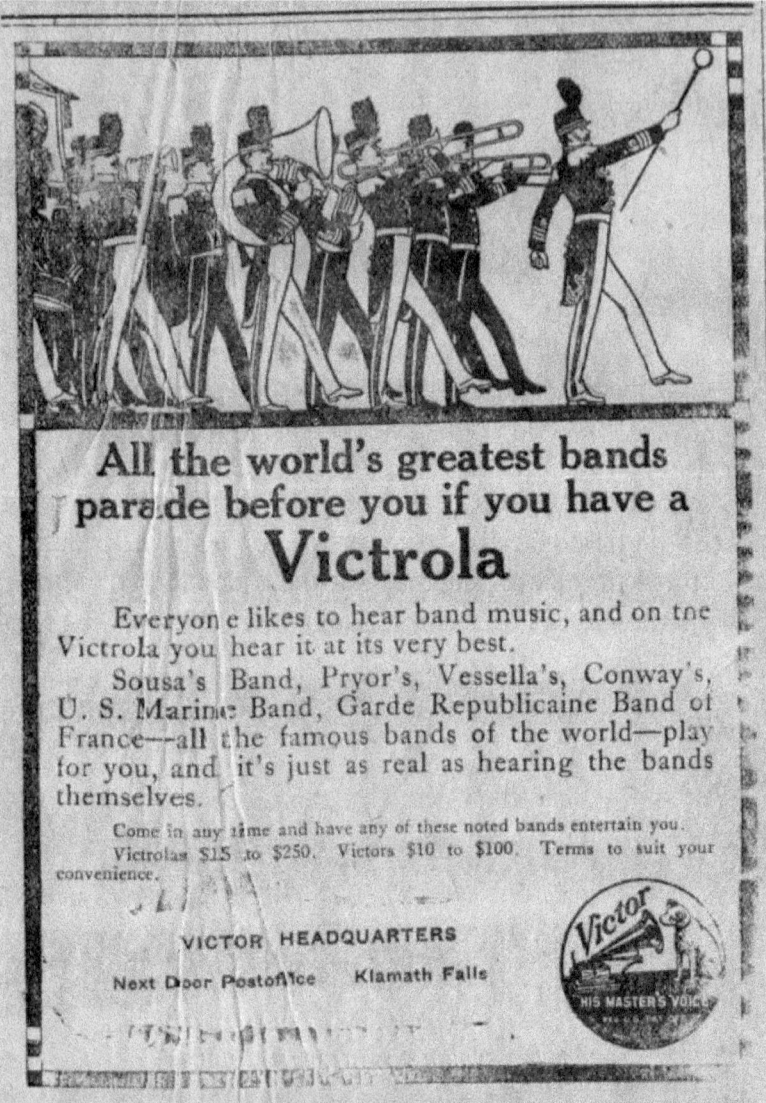

Victrola Advertisement
Evening Herald, 07-03-1916

Conclusion: The Importance of Local Bands in Klamath History

Though the names, appearances, and other features of these various bands changed throughout time, one thing remained constant: the role they all played within the community. These groups were so much more than a chance for entertainment. Rather, they played a unique role in the development of the community. The bands were an excellent opportunity to show off and attract new residents and businesses. These bands were also present for many historical events in the community.

These features continue to this day. Our local music groups are a crucial part of our community, and they especially help create a positive image of Klamath Falls to outsiders. You can be sure that when a person looks at Klamath Falls as a potential candidate for a place to call home or open a new business, our local musical groups provide a positive view of the community that helps attract these individuals.

Local citizens and businesses have always been willing to support these groups for this reason. While weekly concerts or music programs for special holidays are an added bonus, the core mission of these groups has always focused on community building through music. Klamath bands have consistently fulfilled this mission, and many of them have even grown beyond the community to gain status and recognition in the state or region.

What is truly amazing about this feat is that most of these groups consisted of local volunteer talent. While some groups could pay for a bandleader, equipment, sheet music, and other necessities, band members typically offered their services as a courtesy to their community. That these organizations could achieve such levels of success based on volunteer work from these musicians is a testament to these individuals and their dedication to community. This talent and dedication are features that have always existed in Linkville/Klamath Falls and still do to this day.

The next time you see a community group providing music for a local event, you might think about the number of hours that were contributed (especially on a volunteer basis) to make the music happen and about the history of this beloved pastime. These community efforts are woven into our history and are a part of who we are. This is another reason it is so important to support our local musical institutions, even if just by attending their performances. It would be a tragedy if we lost our connection to the vital American tradition that is the local community band.

So, remember, strike up the band! Let the melodies of our past lead us into the future.

FOLLERIN' THE BAND

WHO hasn't "follered" the band up Main street, or up Broadway or Michigan boulevard? Heart pumping joyously, feet beating the ground in time! Grandly intoxicating moment of childhood!

And—later in life—who hasn't felt a thrill as the conductor lifted his baton for the overture to begin? A moment pregnant with the glamour of the theatre! Music casts its spell throughout all the Ages of Man.

Is it wise then, in this enlightened and prosperous day to countenance substitution of a shadow of music for the real thing in the theatre?

Imagine the Irish following a Music Box on St. Patrick's Day! Or fife and drum music by a Machine on Memorial Day! Incongruous? Of course, but not more so than a mechanical overture in the theatre.

Talking pictures—a new dramatic form; the radio—which transmits music directly and DOES reflect the artist's mood of the moment; the phonograph in the home—where living music usually is not available—are not at issue here. We are discussing only the SUBSTITUTION OF MECHANICAL MUSIC FOR REAL MUSIC IN THE THEATRE, in consequence of which Real Music is being eliminated in theatres.

THE AMERICAN FEDERATION OF MUSICIANS

(Comprising 140,000 professional musicians in the United States and Canada)
JOSEPH N. WEBER, President, 1440 Broadway, New York, N. Y.

Follerin' the Band
Klamath News, 11-26-1929

www.ingramcontent.com/pod-product-compliance
Lightning Source LLC
Chambersburg PA
CBHW051405290426
44108CB00015B/2158